SEASONS IN THE SOUTH

The lives involved in the death of General Van Dorn

Linda Gupton

AuthorHouse™
1663 Liberty Drive
Bloomington, IN 47403
www.authorhouse.com
Phone: 1-800-839-8640

© 2013 Linda Gupton. All rights reserved.

No part of this book may be reproduced, stored in a retrieval system, or transmitted by any means without the written permission of the author.

Published by AuthorHouse 6/10/2013

ISBN: 978-1-4817-5366-1 (sc)
ISBN: 978-1-4817-5364-7 (hc)
ISBN: 978-1-4817-5365-4 (e)

Library of Congress Control Number: 2013909500

Any people depicted in stock imagery provided by Thinkstock are models, and such images are being used for illustrative purposes only. Certain stock imagery © Thinkstock.

This book is printed on acid-free paper.

Because of the dynamic nature of the Internet, any web addresses or links contained in this book may have changed since publication and may no longer be valid.

The views expressed in this work are solely those of the author and do not necessarily reflect the views of the publisher, and the publisher hereby disclaims any responsibility for them.

Dedication

Glenda Faye Poarch Reid

Who traveled, gave advice, shared enthusiasm, and used all her English teacher skills to assist in completing this book.

Acknowledgements

Researching a true story cannot be complete without the aid of many individuals in various places. When no cooperation was expected in meeting family members, they were exceptionally kind and generous with their information although at times it was not the most pleasant and complimentary. Laura Willins Walker of Memphis, Tennessee, was the last living granddaughter of Medora Peters Lenow and remembered her well. She shared information about the family that gave awareness about the true nature of their personalities. She was looking forward to reading the completed manuscript; unfortunately, she passed away within the next year after the interview.

An interview in Yazoo City Mississippi with Holly, Rosemary, and Butch Harper, who is a great grandson of Jessie and Dr. Peters, revealed that they were probably the last residents of the plantation home in Arkansas. They are expecting the complete story would tell the next generation about their ancestors.

Barbara N. Cope is a direct descendant of one of General Earl Van Dorn and Martha Goodbread's children. She shared her research, photographs, and support when she should be completing her own manuscript about the family.

David Wakefield found information that no one else had encountered. He declared that he had a very strong interest in the family but had no intention to write the story. His encouragement and research skills were astounding.

Suzy Keasler, Marianna, Arkansas, assisted in finding information about Dr. Peters' children in the local library. She had written about them that are included in the history of Lee County. Pat Wilson and other ladies in the courthouse of Lee County facilitated in finding court records. With the assistance of those in the Helena library and courthouse, courthouse records were found to verify and correct information.

The Maury County, Tennessee, Archives was an invaluable source with court records, references, and family papers. Bob Duncan and Michelle Cannon are priceless when researching especially to those interested in genealogy.

Don Gibson and Andrew Sherriff of Rippavilla Plantation, home of Jessie McKissack's sister Susan, were very supportive in finding information and photographs.

My deepest appreciation to all of these and others so numerous that it would be impossible to name individually.

Table of Contents

The McKissack Family and the Beginning of Spring Hill, Tennessee	1
Dr. George Boddie Peters Early Life	13
The War and the Effects on the Families	33
General Earl "Buck" Van Dorn	41
General Van Dorn and Jessie Peters	59
General Van Dorn's Funeral and Aftermath	71
Dr. Peters' Grown Children	93
General Van Dorn's Families and Children	111
Recovery After the War	117
The Southern Claims Commission	125
Dr. Peters' Last Years	143
Jessie's Last Years With Her Family	155
Medora's Last Years and Her Family	175
Family Tree	197
Epilog	207

The McKissack Family and the Beginning of Spring Hill, Tennessee

Located just 30 miles south from Nashville, Tennessee at the edge of Maury and Williamson Counties, Spring Hill began to develop about the time as the county seat of Columbia. The area of today was much as it was 200 years ago until General Motors announced in 1985 that they would be building the Saturn plant in that vicinity. The building was constructed around the hills and valleys so as not to disturb the agricultural landscape. Businesses located around the small village rather than considering Columbia as a better locale. All of the progress came to a halt in June 2009 when GM announced that they were filing for bankruptcy and idled the plant in Spring Hill among others. Although currently there are employees working in the plant making engines and periodic announcements are conveyed, the future of the establishment is quite uncertain.

The family that was to become so well known in the community of Spring Hill changed the course of history through personal and related decisions about their individual lives. Incidents occurred that families did not discuss outside the family, and when asked, they would exchange few words if any. The way of life in this vicinity began with William McKissack, who was born in Caswell County, North Carolina on November 14, 1781. At the age of 33, he married Rebecca Sallard, but their marriage ended with her death six years later.[1] They had one daughter Eleanor Washington, who later married Orville McKissack, the son of Archibald, William's brother. It was said that William became so distressed over her marriage that he never forgave her. The anguish may have been due to a lawsuit between William and Archibald over slaves. When William was very ill and not expected to live, Eleanor went to see her father, but he turned his head to the wall when she came close to him.[2]

William may have continued to have a great deal of animosity towards Eleanor and Orville because of the court case brought by them seeking possession of certain slaves. When Eleanor was a baby, Charles Sallard, her mother's father, gave William three slaves by the name of Murphy, Anna, and Patsy upon "the condition and with the understanding that said Negroes together with their increase would belong to the said Eleanor W. upon her coming of age or marriage." When Eleanor married Orville in 1833, her father refused to give them the slaves, "but now holds the same claiming as his own." They charged that William McKissack "always and up to the time of the marriage…admitted that the title to said Negros was not in him but that he had them under said agreement with said Sallard. On September 23, 1841, Sallard conveyed the slaves to the complements in a deed of gift," so they now contend that they "have a complete title." The plaintiff requested the slaves and compensation for their hire while in William McKissack's possession. The result indicated that the decision was granted, appealed, and reversed.[3]

However, since there was no will, Eleanor inherited the house in which her father lived that was said to be the first brick home in

---

1 McKissack Bible in possession of Mrs. J. L. Donoho, Copied and furnished for Bible Records in Maury County.
2 Judith Parham Scoville, descendent of Lucy McKissack Parham, personal recollections of family sent to Susan Cheairs' descendent, January 27, 1974, p.1
3 Maury County, Tennessee, Chancery Court Records, Petition #21484203, Filed May 20, 1836.

Spring Hill. Eleanor and Orville were very devoted to each other and gave land for the Episcopal Church to be built in Spring Hill. The land had been a part of the garden of Eleanor's stepmother. At one time a letter came from Scotland indicating that lands, a title, castle, and other things were available for the oldest McKissack. Orville was asked why he did not go and attend to the property, but he responded, "I wouldn't leave Ell for the whole of Europe."[4]

Soon after the death of his first wife, William married Jeanette Susan Cogle Buxton Thomson, daughter of Susanna Peters and Dr. James Thomson, who came to this country from Edinburgh, Scotland. Susanna was now married to William's brother Dr. Spivey McKissick (He always used this spelling.), a graduate of William and Mary but did not practice in Maury County.[5] William and Jeanette had eight children; the first five being born in Person County, North C arolina. Their youngest was the beautiful but defiant Jessie Helen whose colorful life would have a story all her own.

The brothers also had two sisters, Susan and Rebecca, who remained in the Giles County area south of Maury County where their parents settled. The McKissack boys were, as a rule, tall and slender, honest and industrious. They were excellent musicians especially on the violin. It was remembered by some when six sons and the older McKissacks all played their violins at once.[6] Susan married George Simmons and Rebecca married Wilson Jones before the family left Person County North Carolina. Their grandson Calvin E. Wilson was one of the six men who met in the office of his father Judge Thomas M. Wilson and organized the Klu Klux Klan in Pulaski in 1865.[7]

---

4   Letter from Jessie Peters on file with Parham, McKissack, Coleman, Pope, Peters, Cheairs, Van Dorn Families, Spring Hill, Tennessee Public Library Reference, Written about 1900.

5   C. Blair Scoville, "The McKissacks of Maury County," Presented at the Thomas McKissack Chapter, DAR, April 23, 1985, p.1.

6   James T. McKissack, "History of the McKissick (McCusick) Family," Spring Hill, Tennessee Library, April 23, 1935.

7   *Op. Cit.*, Judith Scoville.

Dr. Spivey McKissick settled in Spring Hill about 1823 after he purchased a large stock of goods imported from the Virginia estate of John H. Pointer. He had married Susanna Peters Osborn Thomson ten years before in North Carolina, but her parents moved to Spring Hill area that proved to be an enticement for others to follow. Susanna's previous two husbands were very wealthy men, and when she married Spivey, she was almost twenty years older than he was. Her granddaughter Jessie described her as wearing silk velvet when she traveled and Colonel Jeffries, her first husband, was one of the wealthiest men in North Carolina.

After Spring Hill was incorporated in 1824, Spivey was the first mayor and was joined by William to become leading merchants in the area. He was a builder of the Franklin and Columbia Turnpike, and at the beginning of the War Between the States, Spivey was noted in Tennessee history for purchasing the first Confederate Government bonds for $3,000 that would be equal to over $70,000 by today's standards. Later in the War, the Federal Army passed through Spivey's property on its way to the Battle of Franklin.[8]

Susannah died in 1840, and two years later Spivey was taken to court by Thomas P. Thompson and Harriet Jeffers, Susannah's children by her first two husbands, concerning ownership of slaves. Several in the family and others who had done business with the McKissicks specified that Susannah had handled transactions with them without any interference by Spivey. John Cheairs indicated that for the previous seven years, Spivey had complained of dyspeptic affection. It was a condition of the stomach that causes loss of appetite, nausea, pain in the upper abdomen, heartburn, but usually indigestion. Spivey could not transact business if it required much physical effort, but in spite of everything, he never allowed his wife to transact any of his business.[9]

The same year of the court action, Spivey married Eliza Smizer.

---

8   *Op. Cit*, Blair Scoville. p. 2.
9   Thompson, Thomas P., and Harriet Jeffers vs. Spivey McKissack, Chancery Court, Legal Depositions 88-21, August 6,1842, Spring Hill, Tennessee.

Their only child to live to adulthood was Lucy Ann who moved into her father's property known as Woodlawn and completed the construction of the Woodlawn house. It was known for its hospitality and extravagant furnishings that were imported from England. The interior had stone vestibule with colored marble flooring to the French marble fireplaces. In some of the formal rooms were elaborate medallions with garlands and cherubs. The stairway led all the way to the third floor. It was nothing unusual for city visitors to spend all summer with as many as twenty-five people eating the good country food, riding the good saddle horses, and enjoying the lavish generosity.[10]

In one story, Susan McKissack Cheairs was crying to Lucy about the money that she and Nathaniel owed them. When asked how much it was, Susan responded, "$10,000." Lucy reacted with, "If that is all you are crying about, forget it." The debt was forgotten.[11]

William developed a commercial brick kiln and yard, and his business interests in Maury and many surrounding counties made him extremely successful. When he built his remarkably outstanding house in the early 1840s in the downtown area of Spring Hill, he made his own bricks. By 1850 William was considered a thrifty man with a sharp business ability and regarded as the wealthiest man in the area.[12]

William always taught a trade to the slaves that he owned. By the 1850 US Slave Schedule, he had 34 with an equal number of males and females. The two oldest were 68 and 69 year old men with 12 under the age of 5. One was Moses who was born in 1790 near Raleigh, North Carolina, and was a part of the West African Ashanti tribe in Ghana. In 1822, he married Mirian, a Cherokee, and they had fourteen children. He learned to be a carpenter and woodworker while his brothers were learning the trades of bricklaying, brick making, stone masonry, and lime making. At

---

10 *Op. Cit.*, Blair Scoville.
11 *Ibid.*
12 *Ibid.* p. 3.

least one was trained as a metal worker including the shaping of iron, copper, and brass, and the handling of sheet metal for both roofs and utensils. They would often serve as foremen, superintendents, and overseers and learned to be master builders by being faced with challenging construction and design problems.[13]

Moses was physically enslaved; nevertheless, he used the implements of the building trade to become a skilled craftsman. His ninth child, Gabriel Moses, continued in the building trade that he learned from his father. In his later years, he would tell his and his brothers experiences working on the Maxwell House Hotel in Nashville, the Cheairs, homes in Spring Hill (Nathaniel having married William's daughter Susan Peters McKissack), and other historic residences and public buildings.

During the War Between the States, Gabriel and several of his brothers would join the Union Army. William was listed in the Co. E 12th Regiment US Colored Infantry as 5'8" of dark complexion, eyes, and hair, born in Pulaski, and occupation was servant. After the war, the brothers returned to Nashville to find their parents, who were now elderly, troubled, and with family ties broken. With a great deal of difficulty, they attempted to reunite their family; however, Moses died on August 26, 1865, just four months after the war ended, and Miriam followed four months later after her husband. Both of them are buried in the old City Cemetery on Fourth Avenue South in Nashville.[14]

The War was over, the South was wrecked, buildings destroyed, and the fields were bare. The African American McKissacks had the skills that were needed to rebuild the area. Gabriel went to Pulaski, about 40 miles south of Spring Hill, where he planned to stay for a short period of time; on the other hand, after the chance meeting of a young lady by the name of Dolly Ann, who became his wife, he stayed for the balance of his life. When Moses II began his business in Pulaski, builders were usually designing their own structures.[15]

---

13   "Moses McKissack, Architect and Master Builder," A & I State College cafeteria, Testimonial Banquet, May 11, 1950.
14   *Ibid.*
15   *Ibid.*

Like his father, Gabriel, Moses II taught the building skills to his son Moses McKissack III and Calvin, who were two of seven sons. Moses III was born in Pulaski and received his education in the segregated public schools. He started working for his father, but in 1890 just one year from graduation, he dropped out of the Pulaski Colored High School. That same year, James Porter, a white Pulaski architect, hired him to draw, design, and assist in his construction business. Moses' ingenuity in the trade earned him the reputation as an excellent craftsman. He was a construction superintendent who was building houses for five years in Athens and Decatur, Alabama; Mt. Pleasant and Columbia, Tennessee. He became a construction supervisor at Vale Rolling and Riverburg Mills where he prepared shop drawings for B. F. McGrew and Pitman & Patterson. His proficiency and good judgment in construction earned Moses the reputation as an excellent artisan.[16]

Moving to Nashville in 1905, Moses started his own architectural and construction business in the Napier Court Building. He built a residence for Vanderbilt University's Dean of Architecture and Engineering that led to commissions to design and build other residences in Nashville's West End area including Governor A. H. Roberts. His first major commission was for the Carnegie Library at Fisk University for which Secretary of War William Howard Taft laid the cornerstone. The structure was one of the first in America designed by an African American architect.[17]

By 1909, Moses was one of eighteen architects in Nashville; despite the fact that he advertised in the *Nashville City Directory* as a "colored architect." Three years later he branched to Shelbyville by designing the Administration Building for Turner Normal and Industrial Institute. He also designed dormitories for Lane College in Jackson as well as Nashville's Roger Williams University. By 1920

---

16 Jessie Carney Smith, Millicent Lownes Jackson, and Linda T. Wynn, "McKissack and McKissack Architects and Engineers, Inc." *Encyclopedia of African American Business: K-Z*, (Westport, CT: Greenwood Publishing Group, Inc. 2006), p. 507.

17 *Ibid.*, p. 508.

Moses was designing buildings for clients throughout Nashville and the state. His brother Calvin Lunsford McKissack assisted on most projects. They offered a staff of contracting services with a number of masons, carpenters, and laborers.[18]

Calvin had been studying at Barrows School in Springfield, Massachusetts, for three years when he started attending Fisk University. Through the International Correspondence School in Scranton, Pennsylvania, he eventually received a certificate in architecture. He had been in Nashville the first of four years when Moses established the business in Nashville. Calvin started his own practice in Dallas, Texas, designing numerous churches and schools but returned to Nashville in 1915 to teach architectural drawing at Tennessee Agricultural and Industrial State Normal School today known as Tennessee State University. Directing the Industrial Arts Department of Pearl High School, he became the first executive secretary of the Tennessee State Association of Teachers in Colored Schools that he held until 1922 when he resigned to join his brother.[19]

The state professional registration law became effective in 1921, and the McKissacks were among the first registered architects with Certificates No. 117 and 118. A year later, Calvin Lunsford joined Moses as a partner making McKissack and McKissack Architects and Engineers, Inc., the first in Tennessee to become a professional African American architectural firm. Within three years, the architectural enterprise gained the attention of America's largest denominational conventions. In 1924 the National Baptist Convention, U.S.A, Inc., gave them the contract to design and build the Morris Memorial Building on Charlotte Avenue. Housing the Sunday School Publishing Board, it was the largest building constructed in Nashville up to that time and by local talent. It was capable of publishing the large volume of religious literature for the

---

18 *Ibid.*
19 Elmore, Mary Eloise. "McKissack & McKissack Negro Architects and Builders." Tennessee State College, Senior Project, Tennessee State University Library, 1943. *African American Architects: A Biographical Dictionary 1865-1945, (New York: Routledge 2004), p. 299.*

denomination. Noted for their church edifices, they also received municipal contracts to design a number of educational facilities.[20]

The depression affected them as it did everyone who was struggling financially, but the firm was able to design and build public schools and received numerous Public Works Administration contracts. By 1941, Alabama granted the business a license followed by Georgia, South Carolina, Florida, and Mississippi. A year later the federal government awarded the contract to design the Ninety-ninth Pursuit Squadron Air Base in Tuskegee, Alabama, a World War II African American combat air unit. The contract was looked on as the largest contract ever awarded an African American at the price of $5,700,000[21]

That same year, Moses and Calvin received the Spaulding Medal from President Roosevelt. The award was named for Charles Clinton Spaulding, the founder and first president of North Carolina Mutual Life Insurance Company, the largest African American owned insurance company in America. The award honored the "Outstanding Negro Business" in the country.[22]

The business was involved in the design of several community housing developments, and because of this, President Roosevelt appointed Moses III to the White House Conference on Housing Problems. Other generations continued with the business including the women who were professional engineers. In 1987, the Tennessee Building Commission awarded McKissack and McKissack the design for the National Civil Rights Museum in Memphis.[23]

The business was headquartered in Nashville until it moved to Philadelphia in 2001. It continues with the McKissack women carrying on the family tradition with satellite offices in Tennessee, Washington, D.C., and New York.[24] In recognition of the contributions made by the McKissack brothers to the

---

20 *Op. Cit.*
21 *Op. Cit.* Jessie Carney Smith, p. 509.
22 *Op. Cit*, Elmore, p. 382.
23 *Op. cit.*, Jessie Carney Smith, p. 509.
24 *Ibid.*

historic building heritage of the United States, the National Park Service of the U.S. Department of the Interior listed several of the McKissacks' Nashville buildings in the National Register of Historic Places. Moses McKissack Middle School and McKissack Park were named in honor of Moses III by the Nashville officials for his contributions.[25]

William McKissack, Jessie Peters' father. His brick kiln provided brick for most of the brick houses in Spring Hill. Photo courtesy of Rippavilla Plantation. Spring Hill, TN.

Lucy Ann McKissick, daughter of Spivey, married Thomas Gibson. When Susan McKissack Cheairs was concerned about a $10,000 debt owed her cousin, Lucy told her to forget it. Photo courtesy of Rippavilla Plantation, Spring Hill, TN.

---

25 Linda T. Wynn, *Notable Black American Women*, Book II, (Gale Research Ink: Detroit, MI 2006), p. 452.

Mirian and Moses McKissack brought by William McKissack from North Carolina. Moses learned carpenter and wood worker trades while his brothers learned other trades. Photo courtesy of Anne McKissack Brown, Pulaski, TN.

Gabriel, 9th child of Moses and Marian, and Dolly Ann McKissack. He was in building trades in Pulaski, TN. Photo courtesy Anne McKissack Brown, Pulaski, TN.

Children of Gabriel and Dolly Ann McKissack. Back row from right are Calvin and Moses III McKissack, first African Americans to receive architect licenses. Photo courtesy Ann McKissack Brown, Pulaski, TN.

Dr. George Boddie Peters Early Life

Infants and underage James and Lucy Parker Peters were each less than eighteen when they married on March 29, 1768, with permission on their wedding day from both of their fathers.[26] By 1790, James owned 1200 acres in Wake County North Carolina, had four daughters, three sons, and twenty-two slaves.[27] Within fifteen years, they had migrated to Maury County Tennessee where they were a few of the early settlers in the northern area. A cabin was built above the large spring and grounds about 1814, and a church was established that was referred to as Zion Meeting House.

After the Peters bought the cabin, James started the Methodist camp grounds with meetings that would last for days attracting people who would travel from miles away to attend.[28] Meetings would last for days at a time when many speakers would give their interpretation of the Bible. Families would camp in tents and wagons for these events just to be able to be involved in these enthusiastic and stimulating religious activities and social events. Rev. Thomas

---

26 Permission to marry recorded in Sussex County Virginia on March 29, 1768.
27 Land records in Wake County North Carolina and 1790 Census records.
28 *The Goodspeed Histories of Maury, Williamson, Rutherford, Wilson, Bedford & Marshall Counties of Tennessee,* (Woodward & Stinson Printing Co.: Columbia, TN, 1971), p. 774.

Maddin, the first minister of the Columbia Methodist Church, wrote in 1868 about his experience of preaching four times in the 1820 gathering.[29]

About 1814, George Boddie Peters, son of James P. and Rebecca Boddie Peters, was born in Nash County, North Carolina. His mother's family came from a fine English family dating back to 1612. Her father had been a member of the State Senate of North Carolina from Nash County.[30] Within a year, the family soon followed others to Maury County where their older children spent their young years growing up in the Spring Hill area with their grandparents.

It was suggested that the area be called Petersburg, in honor of James Peters, but he objected based on a passage that he said was in the Bible that stated "Do not name your lands by your own name." It was said that for sixteen years he would take his wooden bucket and tell everyone, "I'm going over to the spring hill and get some water." The area was referred to as Spring Hill ever since 1825.[31]

The first "physician of importance" listed in Spring Hill was Dr. John Hancock Crisp who was born in Caswell County, North Carolina, in 1799, the same county as many of the McKissack family and many of the early residents. He was a graduate at 26 of Philadelphia Medical College that was known in later years as Jefferson Medical College, and he became known as a man of high attainments.[32] He moved to Maury County, Tennessee, soon after graduation in 1825 and married three years later his first wife Mary Jones known as "Polly." Within another three years, they had moved to Gibson County, Tennessee where his wife died in

---

29 D. P. Robbins, *Century Review, 1805-1905*, p. 125.
30 John Thomas Boddie, *Boddie and Allied Families*, United States: Privately printed 1918), p. 98.
31 Larry L. Miller, "Spring Hill," *Tennessee Place Names*, (Indiana University Press: Bloomington: 2001), p. 196.
32 Frederick M. Culp and Mrs. Robert E. Ross, *Past & Present Gibson County*, (Gibson County Historical Society: 1961), p. 30.

1834. He soon married Mary Kennon Smith who was also known as "Polly" although some references indicate "Kennie."[33]

The first physician in Trenton, Tennessee, was John H. Chrisp, who located in Gibson County soon after it was established. He continued to practice there for many years and trained other young men in the profession. William K. Love was a student under Chrisp and later a partner until the mid 1840s.[34] In the history of Gibson County, Tennessee, George B. Peters obtained his professional education in the office of Chrisp & Love. About 1850, Dr. Peters was living in Hardeman County, and Dr. Crisp moved there for a period of time before moving to Mississippi. His second wife died, and he married again to Mary Robert Harwell also known as "Polly." He decided to move to Texas, but Polly refused to go with him. Dr. Crisp went anyway to the Colorado County area and promptly divorced her.[35]

After the war in 1865, Dr. Crisp became so upset with the manner in which the Army was handling reconstruction that he moved to South America with several other families.[36] He had been involved in a lawsuit with the Freedman's Bureau and two of their northern friends in Colorado County, Texas. They ended with all of his material wealth leaving him broke.[37] On March 10, 1868 in a letter to his son James in Columbus, Texas, he relates how he has been destroyed by the "Yankee Government." The Bureau agent had trumped up a bogus claim so that they could get his crops and sell it for themselves.[38]

---

33 "Dr. J. J. Crisp and Dr. John Hancock Crisp," Gibson County, Tennessee, tn-roots, photos.
34 *History of Tennessee*, Nashville, Tennessee, 1886, p. 804.
35 Colorado County, Texas, District Clerk, Records, November 7, 1861, Vol. C2, p. 323-327.
36 Frederick M. Culp—Mrs. Robert E. Ross, *Gibson County, Past and Present,* (Gibson county Historical Society: 1961), p. 309.
37 Online archives, Terry's Texas Rangers. Preserving history of 8th Texas Cavalry Regiment 1861-1865. Incorporated by State of Texas, 1994.
38 Gibson County, Tennessee Genealogy and History posting by Cat Edwards of Crisp letter dated March 10, 1868.

His passport application gives a description of him on August 8, 1865, as 5'8 ¼," blue eyes, gray hair, fair complexion, and a full face. He wrote five years later to his son James, who became a physician in Trenton, that his crops were good in Sao Paulo, Brazil. Of his three other sons who were born in Mississippi, only Alexander was with him. It was very difficult for a man of his age to plant crops, but at 74, he continued to try to make more money since he lost everything in Texas because of the War.[39] When he died in 1888, he was buried in Campo Cemetery in Brazil that had been established by Confederate Colonel Asa Oliver for his daughter who died from tuberculosis. The local priest would not allow any of them to be buried in the municipal burial ground because they were Protestants. Colonel Oliver buried his daughter upon a hill located on his plantation. Allowing others to be buried in the same area, the cemetery became quite large and is visited today by decedents of the Confederates.[40] His obituary indicated that when he died, he had been confined to bed with rheumatism the last five years of his life.[41]

Dr. Peters arrived in Hardeman County in the 1830s and became a prominent physician of high standing in west Tennessee. In May of 1839, he married nineteen year old Narcissa Williams, daughter of Joseph John Williams, who was a planter. He started acquiring land that same month by buying Lot 20 for $121 near what was then known as the margin of the town of Bolivar.[42]

Dr. Peters' brother Thomas was also living in Hardeman County about this time and had married Ann Eliza Glasgow just two years before. Unfortunately, she died five years later. He was engaged in buying and selling lands in the southwestern states by

---

39 Gibson County, Tennessee Genealogy and History web site, Letters written by Dr. John H. Crisp.
40 Charles Christopher Jackson, "Oliver, Asa Thompson," *Handbook of Texas Online*, Texas Historical Association.
41 Jonathan K. T. Smith, *Nashville Christian Advocate 1897-1899*, 2002.
42 W. W. Matthews, "Dr. George Boddie Peters," *The Bolivar Bulletin and Hardeman County Times*, October 27, 1949.

1833. He bought considerable lands in the northern counties of Mississippi from the Indians who sold their possessions before removal to the trans-Mississippi reservations. When he married, he had a plantation and became a cotton grower. Later he moved to Memphis where he became a real estate broker. As a contractor, he built 35 miles of the Memphis and Charleston railroad and also built levees along the Mississippi River.[43]

Less than a year after marrying Dr. Peters, Narcissa died giving birth to a son named Thomas. Four months later, the baby died at the home of his mother's parents and would be buried near his mother.[44] Engraved on her tomb in the old family burial plot near their home, the last four lines are a tribute to her memory:

> 'Her husband erects this frail tribute
> Of Memory over the best gift of Heaven
> To save from oblivion the spot that shrouds
> The moldering ashes of the dearest creature of earth.[45]

He started buying land again the next year with 20 acres southwest of Bolivar and adjoining the town for $300 and Lots 32 and 33. On July 29, 1841, Dr. Peters married Evelina Louisa McNeal McDowell in Hardeman County although she was born in Maury County. Her parents Thomas and Clarissa Polk McNeal came from Mecklenburg County, North Carolina. Clarissa and James K. Polk shared the same grandfather, and eventually about three years later that grandfather and his family migrated to Bolivar.[46]

On April 24, 1838 Clarissa had married Erasmus McDowell in Bolivar who was also born in Maury County. His family had migrated from Virginia to Maury County where Erasmus was born about 1814. They later moved to Bolivar with their three sons and

---

43 Thomas McAdory Owen, LL.D, *History of Alabama & dictionary of Alabama biography* (Chicago: The S. J. Clark Publishing, Company). p. 1348-1349.
44 *Conservative & Holly Springs Banner*, Obituaries, July 17, 1840.
45 *Op. Cit. Matthews*
46 *Ibid..*

one daughter where most of them spent the rest of their lives in that area.

The U. S. Government made a treaty with the Indians to buy their land, and the proceeds would be deposited to a common tribal treasury. Since they were being relocated, the funds would assist them in purchasing lands in the West. The Indians did not really own the lands on which they resided because they believed that ownership belonged to the gods.[47] The land in turn was then sold to individuals, and they were given a patent or conveyance document that was signed by President Martin Van Buren. A land office was established in the district handling the land transactions and Erasmus P. McDowell was a map-maker in the Pontotoc, Mississippi, land office. Four months after his marriage, he had transferred 1,280 acres in Tippah County and over 3,800 acres just in Tate County, Mississippi.[48] It is believed that he died in Mississippi in 1840, but before his death, he had accumulated almost 9,500 acres.

Tillotson McDowell, a brother of Erasmus, had bought land in Tippah County as well but more. He also bought land in Alabama, but his total purchase was almost 2900 acres[49] When Tillotson died in 1873 at the age of 56, he had been the Clerk and Master in the Chancery Court of Bolivar.[50]

Evelina and Erasmus did not have any children; yet, she and Dr. Peters had seven children of whom only four lived to adulthood.[51]

Dr. Peters continued to buy land in 1842, and within seven years, he purchased Square 18 of the original part of Bolivar. One of the sellers was William Reynolds, his neighbor, whose real estate value was twice that of Dr. Peters. He had a cabinet shop on part of the lot in town. Dr. Peters also sold land, and in 1847, he sold

---

47 Thomas Stewart, "From Whence We Came." *The South Reporter*, Holly Springs, Mississippi, April 14, 2005.
48 U. S. Department of Interior, Bureau of Land Management, General Land Office records.
49 *Ibid.*
50 *Whig & Tribune,* Jackson, Tennessee, May 24, 1873.
51 Polk Cemetery Records, Bolivar, Tennessee.

Lot No. 2 of Square No. 8 with a frame building used as a store and occupied by his brother-in-law Samuel W. McNeal. In 1852 he conveyed 436 ½ acres to Matthew A. Trice for $4,360.[52]

Dr. Thomas E. Moore was in practice with Dr. Peters for several years. Born in 1819 in Huntsville, Alabama, he attended schools and academies there, but at the age of 18, he began the study of medicine under his brother Dr. John R. Moore in Greensborough, Alabama. After reading with him for two years, he enrolled in Transylvania University in Lexington, Kentucky. He graduated in 1842 and returned to Alabama but soon made his way to Bolivar. He was recognized over the state as president of the Medical Board and was successful in management of diseases of women and children. By the 1860s, he was over 6' 2 ½ " and weighed over 225 pounds that made him a great deal larger than the average male of that time period. Although his features were strongly marked and a man of force, he was known as a man of much human kindness.[53] He and Dr. Peters were also in business together as they owned jointly the Pleasant Run-Green Roper property.[54]

In the 1850 Slave Schedule, Dr. Peters owned 36 ranging in ages from a few months to 55. He served as a member of the Board of Trustees of the Female Academy of Bolivar, Episcopal Church, and Clinton Lodge No. 54. He made trips over the state making speeches in the interest of Masonry and was considered a most impressive speaker. It was amazing how Dr. Peters was able to accomplish all that he did. It was challenging to be a doctor with only a faithful horse to ride often with no bridges to cross safely, and the danger of wild animals always present as a patient had to be visited.[55]

Evelina died in October of 1855 after losing her youngest child in August and another died a month after her. Within three months, Dr. Peters had lost his wife and the two youngest of his children. He

---

52 *Op Cit. Matthews.*
53 William S. Speer, *Sketches of Prominent Tennesseans* (Genealogical Publishing Co.), p. 312.
54 *Op. Cit.*
55 *Ibid.*

was left with three sons ages 5-13 and a daughter 7. There again, he must have thrown himself into more work as he helped to organize the Hardeman County Medical Society.

The following was copied from *The Nashville Journal of Medicine and Surgery*:

At a meeting of the physicians of Hardeman County, held at Bolivar on the 6th day of April A. D. 1857, for the purpose of organizing a Medical Society, Dr. A. P. Waddell was called to the chair, and Dr. J. S. Burford appointed secretary. On motion it was unanimously resolved that we adopt the constitution of "Davidson County Medical Society" as our constitution.

The Society then proceeded to the election of officers for the current year, whereupon the following gentlemen were put in nomination and elected, viz: For President, George Wood; Vice-President, George B. Peters; Recording Secretary, J. S. Burford; Treasurer, J. R. Westbrook.

The president appointed J. J. Neely, J. R. Westbrook, and H. Black, a committee to draft By-laws for the government of the Society.

On motion the Society unanimously adopted the code of ethics of the "American Medical Association."

The President appointed the following gentlemen to prepare reports on the diseases, respectively assigned them, to be read at the next regular meeting of the society, viz:

Cholera Infantum—J. S. Burford   (*stomach and bowl*)
Intermittent Fever—J. S. Gibson
Typhoid Fever—R. A. Westbrook
Dysmenorrhea—J. J. Neely   (*Painful Menstruation*)
Ulceration—George B. Peters
Prolapsus—T. E. Moore   (*Displacement of colon/uterus*)
Erysipelas—F. N. Brown   (*Skin Infection*)
Pneumonia—H. Black

Scarlet Fever—J. R. Westbrook
Hysteria—A. P. Waddel

Dr. J. S. Burford was appointed delegate to the American

Medical Association to be held in Nashville on the 5th day of May, A. D. 1857. And in case of his failure to attend, R. A. Westbrook and J. A. Gibson were appointed alternates.

Our motion was ordered that the proceedings of this meeting be sent to the Nashville Journal of Medicine and Surgery, and the "Bolivar Democrat" for publication. On motion the Society adjourned to meet again the first Monday in May next.

Geo. Wood, President
Thos. E. Moore, Rec. Secretary[56]

On May 31, 1858, at the age of 44, Dr. George Peters in consideration for a bond of $1,250, obtained a license to marry his cousin, twenty year old Jessie Helen McKissack of Spring Hill, Tennessee, just north of Columbia in Maury County. The marriage bond was to assure the state that the groom was able to be legally married. The marriage bond was enacted in the 1600s because of the scarcity of ministers. The colony required those wishing to marry go to the county court clerk and give bond with sufficient security that there was no lawful cause to prevent the marriage. The amount was usually $150 by the 19th century. No money actually changed hands at the time the bond was issued.[57] Because Jessie's father was deceased, her cousin John W. McKissack signed instead. The next day in the home of her sister and brother-in-law Lucy and William Parham, the couple was married by Right Reverend Pickett of St. James Episcopal Church in Bolivar. They immediately moved to the home of Dr. Peters in the Bolivar area.[58]

Dr. Peters brought four children to this union: Thomas 16, James 12, Clara 10, and George, Jr. 8. Four months later, Thomas applied to enter the University of Mississippi on October 4. Clara would enroll in the Columbia Athenaeum in Columbia, Tennessee.

---

56 *The Nashville Journal of Medicine and Surgery*, Vol. XII, (Nashville: May 1857), p. 375.
57 John Vogt & T. William Kethley, Jr., *Frederick Co., VA Marriage Bonds*.
58 C. Blair Scoville, "The McKissacks of Maury County," Presented at the Thomas McKissack Chapter, DAR, April 23, 1985, p.4.

The Athenaeum was a very prestigious girls school operated by the Reverend Franklin Gillette Smith and his wife Sarah. Bishop James H. Otey established many of the Episcopal churches in Tennessee including the one in Columbia. He met in 1836 with Leonidas Polk, who later was bishop of Louisiana, and some others to discuss the building of the Columbia Female Institute. Rev. Franklin Gillette Smith and his wife Sarah operated a girls school in Lynchburg, Virginia, but were enticed to Columbia two years later to manage the school.[59] They were there fourteen years when they left to start their own institution located just south of the Institute. The curriculum included many courses that only males had the opportunity to study. Although the school was not connected to any particular church, religion played an important part of the school. Every day was started with Bible reading, singing, and kneeling in the student's place for prayers. They were expected to do the same before retiring for the night. Boarding students would attend St. Peter's Episcopal Church adjacent east of the campus unless their families requested that they attend another.[60] Jessie attended the Female Institute until the Athenaeum was established and graduated from the school in 1853.

On December 20 just 6 months and 20 days later of the same year of their marriage, Jessie gave birth to Harry, but he lived only 28 days.

It appears that just shortly after they were married, Dr. Peters had taken issue with Jessie's brother-in-law Nathaniel Cheairs and had written him letters. Nathaniel was in Holly Springs, Mississippi, when he began a letter to Dr. Peters in Bolivar:

> Dear Sir: Your letters one written from Bolivar & the other from Memphis was received by me on yesterday & their contents carefully noted, and I must confess that I am somewhat at a loss to know what construction to put

---

59 Mary Polk Branch, *Memoirs of a Southern woman*, December 1911, pp. 7-8.
60 *The Guardian*, Vol. X, No. 9, 1852, pp. 215-216.

upon a part of your letter from Memphis. You state that if that land matter is settled (I presume you allude to the Hammons tract.) Satisfactorily: you promise me to take no part in any way in annoying me in my administration. Am I to understand that you intend to annoy me either singly or with other persons if the land matter you allude to is not satisfactorily settled; if so I am sorry you have so far mistaken me, or that you have so poor opinion of me, as to think for a moment, that I can be bribed for money, much less a threat of being annoyed in the settlement of an estate, when I have taken a solemn oath to do that thing to the best of my knowledge and ability as to the settlement of Col. McKissack Estate. I have neither sparse time nor trouble to accomplish its settlement and that for the best interest of all concerned—My official acts are & will be a matter of record to be investigated & scrutinized by any & all persons who may desire to do so —and I am conscientious before God and man when I say that in all my business transactions I have had in view the interest of all the heirs for the least prejudice to the estate, all matters that has come before me for settlement and was not fully comprehended by me. I have in every case got legal advice as to how to proceed.

All this I have done, and in so doing, I have sacrificed nearly all of my home comforts of the association of my wife and children in which is no small share of my happiness-- besides all this, my personal property has suffered no small loss for the want of my personal property has suffered no small loss for the want of my attention, and now to be (if not directly) indirectly threatened with annoyance unless certain matters of land is satisfactorily settled, and it is not only a threat but it is accusing me of being the cause of the difficulty you allude to—now if I am to be blamed for all the wrongs (if there are any) not only for myself but for all the heirs at law. I think it is high time for me to change my position to say the least of it I occupy a very unenviable position.

As to the Hammons trust land, that is to let you and Jessie take it at $40 per acre. I told you if all the rest were willing I was. You told me that you had got the consent of James, Orville, and Parham & that you intended to write to Alex.

I also stated to you on the corres. that I would not consent for you to take it at the $40 unless you & Jessie intended to improve it and live on it—that I was unwilling for you to take the land at $40 & turn around & sell it at $50. I said to you that I did not think it right for 4 or 5 of us to bind ourselves in an obligation not to let the real estate property by sacrificed & then after making the property bring the highest figure & becoming responsible to the estate, for said property for us to give up that property with all of its increase to one who took no part of the responsibility to make a speculation.

It is true as I told you on the corres. that I bought the land for Jessie— & some few months afterwards, she refused to take it thereby throwing the land upon me, to be paid for the best way. I could---suppose that land had depreciated 10 or 20 percent from cost, do you think Jessie would insist on taking it or would you want to take it. Don't infer from the last sentence that I am opposed to her taking if her brothers & sisters are willing. I am entirely so—but as I said to you again I intend to throw the whole responsibility of that matter up on them.[61]

The letter was not signed, but from the content, it must be created by Nathaniel Cheairs, who was the administrator of William McKissack's estate.

December 12, 1858, just eight days before the birth of their first child, an answer to Dr. Peters' abrupt correspondence was made by Nathaniel:

> Dear Sir Your very learned & elaborate effusion written in an a way to frothy "absolution of egotistic defiance" was received by me last night and as it surpasses my comprehension as far I shant attempt to answer it. I merely write to inform you of its inspection, and to request you to bring with you the "frothy absolution of egotistic defiance" as you say you will be in Spring Hill soon after that you can put it in a quilt frames of lace in your parlor. I am surprised

---

61 Figuers Collection, Addition 1830-1964, Tennessee State Library and Archives, Microfilm Accession Number 1153.

is a start of a fool, a darn mad or maniac, could emblazon a thing upon paper that would call forth so much learning.[62]

Jessie was infuriated with Nathaniel being appointed to handle her father's estate, and would not be considerate of any decision that he made. She no doubt exerted a great deal of influence on Dr. Peters.

Dr. Peters gave up his medical practice for politics when he was elected to the General Assembly in 1859. Running as a democrat, Dr. Peters won the 33rd General Assembly senate seat to represent Hardeman, McNairy, and Hardin Counties. He virtually retired from medical practice and dedicated himself to farming and politics. Although he and Jessie had moved to Bolivar shortly after their marriage, they would return to Spring Hill when the legislature was in session in Nashville and stay in the house that Jessie inherited. He introduced the first public health bill that was defeated but was brought back the next year and passed.

Records of the 1861 Tennessee Legislature reveal that Dr. Peters was not present on April 30 when the bill to submit a secession ordinance to the people was introduced. Yet on May 1, the record indicates that he appeared and took his seat. He asked and obtained leave to record his vote in the affirmative. This vote was for the passage of Senate Bill No. 1 to submit to a vote of the people, a declaration of the State of Tennessee, and to call a Convention of the State. Additional amendments were also voted in the affirmative by Dr. Peters. When the secession ordinance went to the people, it was passed by a tremendous margin.[63]

Jessie was expecting her third child that year who was born on November 11; a daughter she named Lucy Mary.

Dr. Peters' two oldest sons would leave the schools that they were attending to return home to fight for the Confederacy. Thomas McNeal entered the University of Mississippi in October 1858 as

---

62 Letter located in the files of Rippavilla Plantation, home of Susan McKissack and Nathaniel Cheairs.
63 The Mysteries of Spring Hill, Tennessee" *Blue & Gra Magaziney*,(Columbua, OH: October-November 1984), p. 13.

a sophomore. The university began just ten years earlier when it opened its doors to eighty students. It is not known if he transferred from another institution or had the academic aptitude to progress to this level. Records do not indicate a declared major, but courses include moral philosophy, chemistry, Latin, Greek, mathematics, and logic. He was a brilliant student and was number one in his junior and senior class. He had few absences from such regular student activities as prayers and recitation and was a member of Delta Psi by the next year after entering the university.[64]

More than likely, Burton Harrison, an assistant professor of physics, was his teacher or they knew each other. Harrison left the university the next year to go to Richmond and serve as the private secretary of Confederate President Jefferson Davis. His father and Jefferson Davis had been very good friends and wanted him to be on the faculty of the University of Virginia in Charlottesville. However, his father went to Louisiana and passed the bar but died when Burton was about three.[65] The Smiths contacted his mother to be a teacher at the Columbia Athenaeum School for Girls in Columbia. Sarah Davis Smith was related to Burton's father. Burton's sister attended the school that allowed young men of the staff to attend. Burton lived in Columbia until about the age of twelve when he left to live with his mother's brother who was a Methodist minister.[66]

Listed as being from New Orleans, William C. Nelson was a classmate of Thomas. His father was an inspector of insurance underwriters, and the family had moved several times. When he wrote his mother in Holly Springs, Mississippi, in May 1860, he told her that he had not received the clothes that his father had promised. He also wanted his father to send some money because it would take over $20 for board, $6 for washing, and about $35 in all. He did

---

64 John R. Wall, Library Specialist, Archives and Special Collections, J. D. Williams Library, The University of Mississippi, January 8, 2009.

65 Library of Congress, Mississippi Division, Stanton Papers, Letter from Fort Delaware, Del., January 12, 1866.

66 Frank H. Smith, *History of Maury County, Tennessee*, Notes Compiled by Maury County Historical Society, 1969, p. 262.

not want them to think that he was extravagant and cared little for the party that everyone was expected to subscribe to whether they went or not. He pointed out that they knew Thomas Peters, and he had already spent $400 and was not extravagant, but he had a right to spend money since he stood first.[67]

The 1861 Senior Class Book highlights the school just prior to the War. Students at the university during this time were subject to extreme regimentation from sunrise until the 9 pm curfew. The faculty checked students' rooms at least once a day, and the sale of liquor was forbidden within five miles of campus. The strict regulations caused many students to be suspended.[68]

President and Chancellor Frederick Augustus Porter Barnard attempted to reorganize the university and its methods of operation to create a more demanding academic institution. He was not able to enact all his plans, but he created separate departments for physics, chemistry and mathematics.[69]

During the spring of 1861 political events interrupted campus activities. Many of the students withdrew before the school term to join the Confederate Army. Realizing that the War would continue indefinitely, all the faculty resigned. The school closed when only four students registered in the fall and did not reopen until after the War. Many of the students joined the University Greys and were lost at the Battle of Gettysburg especially during Pickett's Charge. Not a single member was left standing after the assault. This company penetrated the Union lines further than any other, but they were dead, dying, or wounded.[70]

Professor Alexandre J. Quinche was a native of Minnesota but remained at the university. He was made custodian of the university

---

67 Jennifer W. Ford. *The Hour of Our Nation's Agony*, (The University of Tennessee Press: 2007), p. 11.
68 *University of Mississippi 1861 Senior Class Book*, Introduction, Archives & Special Collections, University of Mississippi, 2004.
69 *Ibid.*
70 "The First Years of the University," The University of Mississippi, School of Engineering.

building and more than likely saved the school from the Union soldiers. He had lived in Illinois and knew General Grant's relatives. The first Union general to enter Oxford, Mississippi, was Grant. He placed a guard around the university building, and the protection continued throughout the War.[71]

In 1866 the university held a graduation ceremony for the Class of 1861. Francis A. Pope of Georgetown, Colorado, was the only student who came.[72] He was a member of Delta Psi as Thomas Peters but longer. He received the rank of captain while he fought for the Confederacy. After the War, he became an attorney and died in New York.[73] All the students were male because women were not admitted until 1882-83 school year.[74]

Thomas Peters left the University of Mississippi to return home and join the Confederate army. At the age of nineteen, he enlisted on May 25 in Bolivar by Capt. M. T. Polk. He entered at Camp Brown about eighty miles north of Bolivar in Union City on August 7, 1861, as a sergeant to Capt. Marshall T. Polk's Light Battery, Corps of Artillery, Tennessee Volunteers for one year. His horse was valued at $130 and equipment at $25. Union City was a large town in the 1860s with thirteen thousand residents. In the early months of 1861, Camp Brown was established one mile north of Union City in preparation for General Leonidas Polk's invasion of Kentucky and occupation of Columbus in September.[75]

Dr. Peters' brother Thomas was living in Memphis when the war broke out. Although he was 49, he was commissioned by the governor of Tennessee as chief quartermaster of the state

---

71 *University of Mississippi, Historical Catalogue of the University of Mississippi 1849-1909*, (Nashville, Tenn.: Marshall & Bruce Company 1910), p. 29.
72 *Op. Cit, 1861Class Book.*
73 Delta Psi Catalog, Faternity of Delta Psi, p. 3,7.
74 *Op. Cit.,Historical Catalogue, p. 10.*
75 R. C. Forrester, "Obion County," *The Tennessee Encyclopedia of History and Culture*, (Nashville, Tennessee: Tennessee Historical Society December 25, 2009).

troops. On a more complete organization of the Confederate States Army, he was commissioned major in the service and assigned to the duties of quartermaster on the staff of Major General Leonidas Polk. He remained in the field in the capacity until the assumption of the command of the army of Tennessee by General John Bell Hood.[76]

The last important engagement in Obion County pitted the United States Seventh Tennessee Cavalry under the command of Colonel Isaac Hawkins against Nathan Bedford Forrest's Seventh Cavalry under the command of Colonel Duckworth. Unable to take the Federal stronghold at Union City by storm, the Confederates devised a "Quaker cannon" from a black painted log and wagon wheels and successfully demanded unconditional surrender in Forrest's name.[77]

Thomas Peter's mother was related to Leonidas Polk and may have influenced his decision to join in this area besides his uncle serving under Polk. By September 5, he was promoted to 2nd Lieutenant. Within the next year, he was apparently having serious medical problems. From May to June 1862, he was absent on the company muster roll under orders of the commanding general.[78]

Dr. Peters' second son, James Arthur, received an appointment to the United States Naval Academy at Annapolis, Maryland, from the 10th Congressional District of Tennessee. He entered the academy on September 20, 1860, at the age of 14 years and 9 months. From December 30 to the following March 1, Midshipman Peters accumulated 24 demerits for delinquencies such as: skylarking (*carouse, disturbing*) in study room, musket not in order, failing to maintain proper discipline in study room, loud talking in study room, disorderly in ranking, and loitering in open desk. The midshipmen in that day were much younger as a rule than those of today. Many were only 14 and very small for their age.

---

76 Thomas McAdory Owen and Marie Bankhead Owen, "Thomas Peters," (Chicago: The S. J. Clark Publishing Company 1921), p. 1348.
77 *Op. Cit.*, Forrester.
78 Thomas M. Peters, Capt. Marshall's Company, Tennessee Artillery, Muster war records.

Numerous students were very sincere and developed friendships among the northern and southern midshipmen. James resigned in March 1861,[79] returned to his home in Tennessee, and eventually joined the Confederate Navy.

When the conflict began, the Union possessed only a limited peacetime fleet while the Confederate Navy was just a figure of speech. Soon the makeshift navies were in a battle over commerce crucial to the Confederacy. The Lincoln administration declared a blockade of much of the Southern coastline, concentrating on major ports: Wilmington, Charleston, and Savannah on the Atlantic coast; and Mobile, New Orleans, and Galveston on the Gulf.

By the ninth of July, James only 15 years old had joined the Confederate Navy as acting midshipman, 3rd class since he had previous service in the United States Naval Academy. He reported for duty on September 14 aboard the side wheeled steam tug *CSS Ellis*[80] that had been bought by North Carolina and had been given to the Confederacy when they joined. The ship was captured at Roanoke Island, North Carolina, in February the next year.[81] James was paroled, and later served aboard the *CSS Atlanta*, Savannah station. This ironclad ram was made in Scotland under another name. In November 1861, she ran the blockade into Savannah, Georgia, with a large cargo of weapons and military supplies. After the Union closed the exists from Savannah preventing her from further use as a blockade runner, she was changed to a casemate ironclad and renamed.[82]

---

79   Dorothea V. Abbott, Special Collections & Archives Department, Vol. 355, 1860-1861, United States Naval Academy, 2009.
80   Thomas Arthur Peters, Confederate States Navy Personnel Index, p. 36.
81   "Ellis," Dictionary of American Naval Fighting Ships, Naval History & Heritage Command, Department of Navy, Navy Historical Center, Washington, DC.
82   "CSS Atlanta," Dictionary of American Naval Fighting Ships, Naval History & Heritage Command, Department of Navy, Navy Historical Center, Washington, DC.

Reverend Franklin G. Smith began the publication of *The Guardian* while he was at the Female Institute and continued when he established the Athenaeum school in Columbia. In February of the 1861 issue, Dr. Peters is listed as a patron from Bolivar. Clara Peters is listed among the students of drawing for the winter examination, and an exhibition of penmanship, drawing, painting, and embroidery would be in the Rotunda. Clara was also listed in third class in Latin as taking their exams on Thursday morning. Parents, friends, and the general public were invited to attend as students would stand before their instructors for the examination.

At 7:00 on Friday evening, the students would perform during a concert.

PROGRAMME

PART I

1. *Quatrieme   Marche   aux   Flambaux*

                                                        Meyerbeer

Clara was among seven students to play the piano.[83]

The War began in April but did not affect the school until the next February when the Yankee troops entered the county. Sixty-four boarding students left in one day on the train as other school students and individuals were trying to reach home. Gentlemen and officers gave up their seats, and many held on to the cow catcher for the young ladies to have a seat. The school never closed; however, Mrs. Smith eventually held classes in the bedroom of her home to as few as eight to twelve students. The school would have been considered abandoned property and taken over by carpet baggers and contraband if the school had officially closed its doors. It also was a functioning school and was, therefore, never converted to a hospital. Soldiers were often camped on the campus, and generals

---

83 *The Guardian*, Vol. 1, No. 2, February 1861.

used the office as headquarters while the Institute next door was used as a hospital.[84]

Although there are twenty-two graduates listed in the graduating Class of 1862, no diplomas were issued. Because Columbia was taken possession by the Union on February 20, most of the students from outside of Columbia left the previous two days.[85] Clara Peters continued to be a student until at least 1863. Only one graduate is listed for 1863 and no graduates are listed in 1864 to 1865. At some point before the War was over, Clara entered the Academy of the Visitation convent in St. Louis, Missouri. Her Mother Superior wrote that Clara came from Bolivar, Tennessee, then endangered by the Civil War.[86]

---

84 Frank Harrison, *Annotations to my Diary*, p. 11.
85 Frank H. Smith, "Graduates 1862," *Graduates of Female Institute and Athenaeum*, p. 89.
86 Sisters of the Visitation, B.V.M, From Monastery of St. Louis, Mo., Nov. 30, 1917.

The War and the Effects on the Families

When the legislature was in session in Nashville, the Peters family lived in Spring Hill in a house that Jessie had inherited from her father. That is not to say that the residents of Bolivar were not aware of Dr. Peters' new wife. Always described as an incredibly beautiful woman and a captivating temptress, Jessie left a lasting impression on the congregation of Bolivar's St. James Episcopal Church. One local account of the parishioners' first glimpse of her was "with plumes flying and silks rustling, Jessie swept into the church leaving the parishioners gasping. Her gown was elegant, her carriage regal, and her companion unbelievable. A black servant trailed behind, and as she paused at the Peters' pew, he quickly spread a large silk handkerchief and with some affectation… as she knew all eyes were focused on her. The servant handed her a small prayer book and left the church. Her entrance never varied, but in time the routine became commonplace that it no longer caused comment. She was always on her shopping trips by a black servant, and made a royal progress."[87] Before the end of 1859, Jessie had another son whom she named William McKissack.

When Jessie was four, her mother died. Sixteen months later,

---

87 "The Mysteries of Spring Hill Tennessee," *Blue & Gray Magazine*, Vol. II, Issue 2, Columbus, OH, October-November 1984, p. 13.

sixty-one year old William married thirty-eight year old Arabella White of Columbia on September 13, 1843. The marriage was brief and lasted about two years. A divorce was very rare, whispered about, or never mentioned in some families. When they went to court, the records referred to the divorce as an agreement and separation. They agreed to "separate and live apart for and during the balance of their lives." Arabella took back eleven slaves, and William agreed to pay her debt to her brother Alexander, who was a judge living in Alabama.[88] Most of William's children continued to live in his house, but he died ten years later. Jessie lost her father when she was seventeen.

Eleanor, who had married Orville McKissack, inherited the brick house since there was no will to indicate any particular specifications. William may have left his first child nothing since he never forgave her for marrying his brother's son. Because there were minor children, Nathaniel Cheairs was appointed administrator of the property much to the dismay of Jessie and her sister Lucy.

Almost ten years later, Tennessee was developing into the second state to have the most battles of the War Between the States. The last of November 1864, Union General John M. Schofield was directing his troops in route for Nashville to avoid his old West Point schoolmate General John Bell Hood's rush forward of the Confederate Army. About dusk, Schofield arrived in Spring Hill and appeared at the McKissack house that he planned to take possession for his headquarters. Eleanor was terrified that her house would be burned, but the general assured her that it would not be, but his troops would probably by surrendered there. About midnight he decided to attempt moving his troops further north towards Franklin in the likelihood that the Confederates had not secured the escape route.[89] Because he was afraid that he would be

---

88 Court Records Agreement between William McKissack and Arabella McKissack and Ephaim W. McRady, Trustee for Arabella McKissack, Filed May 21, 1845.

89 Jill K. Garrett, *Hither and Yon*, The Maury County, Tennessee Homecoming '86 Committee, Second Edition: (Maury County Historical Society1999) p. 193.

captured, General Schofield handed his sword and pistol to Eleanor McKissack and asked that she guard them for him. The plan was successful, and the Union troops arrived in Franklin the next morning in time to prepare breastworks to their advantage in the battle.[90]

Susan McKissack's husband Nathaniel invited Confederate General John Bell Hood and his Army of Tennessee ranking officers to have breakfast at Rippavilla before moving their forces after General Schofield and his Union soldiers. They had apparently passed by them during the night without notice. Seated at the table of fried ham, hot biscuits and steaming coffee were five generals who would be slaughtered before the day ended in the Battle of Franklin: Pat Cleburne, H. J. Granbury, O. F. Strahl, John Adams and "States' Rights" Gist.[91]

The horrific Battle of Franklin started about twelve miles away at 4:30 in the afternoon of November 30, 1864. The small village of Spring Hill was traumatized as houses shook from the discharge of heavy artillery pounding filled the air with a blaring roar. Twenty-five residents rushed for the McKissack house basement as the most secure place to be. A few weeks later, Schofield returned to the McKissack House to reclaim his weapons. The Confederates were in full retreat after being defeated in the Battle of Nashville.[92]

Jessie's oldest sister Susan had married Nathaniel Francis Cheairs on September 2, 1841. It was acknowledged that Jessie resented the fact that her brother-in-law was handling her share of her father's estate. She inherited the house and land where she and Dr. Peters lived while they were in Spring Hill. The McKissack temper was known in the family and Lucy, sister of Jessie and Susan, was confirmed to have been so upset over a share of her

---

90 Frank H. Smith, "Interview with Nathaniel F. Cheairs,"*History of Maury County, Tennessee*, Notes Compiled by Maury County Historical Society, 1969, p. 3.
91 Reid Smith, "Rippaville," *Majestic Middle Tenn*, (Louisiana: Pelican Publishing Company 1998), p. 59.
92 *Op. Cit.* Garrett, p. 192

father's estate in a confrontation with Nathaniel that she kicked him down the steps. Other members of the family describe the McKissacks as a very confrontational, easily upset family.[93]

Although it is not known what the full intent of the following letter is referring, it is in the files of the Cheairs' plantation known as Rippavilla. It was written in March 1862 in Bolivar less than a year after the War began and four years after her marriage to Dr. Peters. Jessie's attitude is very evident throughout the content:

> Mr. Cheairs,
> I have just rec'd a letter from Dr. Peters telling me about your charges. Well upon my words!! Ha! Ha! Seriously Sir you provoke a smile—Why you don't say you'll try to make <u>me</u> pay for what <u>you</u> paid to get out of –A "there are more things in Heaven & Earth than are dreamt of in your philosophy"__. bright__ the wealth of the Indies could not tempt me to pay for the luxury again.
>
> Certainly I don't think I ever spent six months in all at your house—perhaps you allude to my <u>washing</u>—I did have my <u>common</u> clothes washed there and bought my own starch for even those—In the kindness of her heart Aunt Eliza offered her washerwoman services for everything I wanted washed.
>
> I excuse you from blame when in all truth I say that I was thankful to get my bed made once in two weeks and the coldest winter night that ever came a fire was too great a luxury to be dreamed of although wood and negros were plenty. Some have tried to induce the credulous to believe that I am a "tempest" but tempest can easily raft from them enormous matters when <u>pride</u> teaches us forbearance. If people would only read over the commandments once a year they would be considerable edified and learn there from that "the sins of the parents shall be visited on the children.
>
> The one prolix we can be brief I heard my father say before your wife and perhaps yourself were present that the work Wesley done on was doing them was to pay my board

---

93 Judith Parham Scoville, descendent of Lucy McKissack Parham, personal recollections of family sent to Susan Cheairs' descendent, January 27, 1974, p.2.

and his when he was there. We might learn honesty from his paying his board on his deathbed on mothers paying for a corner for his head that was the work of his own slaves. I was led to believe that you had not forgotten it when your sephior as question at the work giving in of what you had rec'd from my brother, that it was a "private understanding between Col. McK & yourself-each and every one of them understand your remark —but perhaps kept them from saying—"yes paying Jess board" I consider that, that dept— has been ten times over liquidated.

    As to attending to my property—I don't think it has been half attended to yet—I know you never troubled yourself about hiring my servants and I know there was nothing else to attend to. I think some of us have paid right dear for our whistles—yes dears than <u>we'll</u> ever know anything about.

    As bad as it frightens me to ride behind 2.4v's in Jim's buggys and as repulsive as the fore is at public houses. I'll go through it all to get 10,000 besides, that will buy what lands for the benefit of our numerous problems not exactly considered within the lawful pale.

    I am glad I have established my reputation for of course we don't expect you to be astonished—but might recall and touch lightly for your hands in as <u>Lion's mouth</u>—I don't allude to—George Peters for his motive is "prudence is the better parts of valour" and he is more prolific than his better half—he never enters difficulties willingly but being in the oppose has better benown of him.

Mrs. Dr. G. B. Peters

Jessie must have returned to Spring Hill soon after the letter was written.

After the fall of Forts Henry and Donelson in northern Tennessee, the Federals were taking over Nashville. Governor Isham Harris had given up governorship of the state when Union troops took Nashville. The General Assembly had adjourned and detached to the Memphis area with the governor and state archives. The state records were packed in 41 boxes, and the state's money consisted to a great extent of Mexican gold placed into 56 boxes and two casks. They were returned to Nashville after William G. Brownlow took office. He and Secretary of State A. J. Fletcher went to the railway station and had the cargo loaded on six army transport wagons. Brownlow mounted himself on the leading wagon in the caravan and seated himself on a box of the archives with a gold-headed walking can in his hand and his feet resting upon a box of the treasure. He drove through the street of Nashville to the cheering multitude of people as he went up the high hill to the capital.[94]

Dr. Peters was in Memphis with the state legislature by the last of February, and the Federals took over Memphis by June preventing many legislators from being able to return home. Union forces had destroyed the Confederate River defenses and occupied Memphis. Without a home, many of the state legislature went into exile in Mississippi, while Governor Harris attached himself to the Army of Tennessee as an Aide-de-camp to Albert Sidney Johnston and Joseph E. Johnston.[95]

Dr. Peters was able to go to his plantation in Council Bend, Arkansas. His vast land holdings in Arkansas had included sixty servants with eleven houses. He would be there a year before returning home. Soldiers were ever present in and around the area although there were no battles near where his property was located. The Battle of Shiloh occurred during April 6-7, 1862 in Hardin County about 40 miles east from Bolivar. Dr. Peters offered his services in amputating limbs and assisting the wounded of either side but was not accepted. He got supplies from federal Generals Hurlbut and Sherman to run his farm since his slaves preferred to stay with him. He would slip away from the rebels and hide in the island when they came to break him apart. They almost caught him

---

94   E. Merton Coulter, *William G. Brownlow: Fighting Parson of the Southern Highlands* (Chapel Hill: North Carolina Press 1937), p. 266.

95   David S. Heidler, Jeanne T. Heidler, and David J. Coles, *Encyclopedia of the American Civil War: A Political, Social, and Military History*, (W. W. Norton & Co.: 2002), p. 1932.

in the middle of the night when he was attending a sick servant but escaped into the orchard and heard what they intended to do.[96]

He decided during early summer that he was going to take the oath of allegiance to the United States after the Federal troops reached Helena, Arkansas just a few miles South of his property and took possession of the Mississippi River. He traveled to Memphis and received consents for protection of his Arkansas property from both Admiral David D. Porter, who commanded gunboat flotilla, and General Ulysses S. Grant. After that time, he dealt in cotton and carried supplies to his neighbors by consent of the military authorities who were commanding in the region.[97]

Nathaniel Francis Cheairs in Confederate uniform during the war, husband of Susan McKissack. Courtesy Rippavilla Plantation, Spring Hill, TN.

Susan McKissack Cheairs, Oct. 31, 1821- June 15, 1893. Jessie Peters' sister. Photo courtesy of Rippavilla Plantation, Spring Hill, TN.

---

96 U. S. National Archives & Records Administration, RG 123, Cong. #3690, George B. Peters Testimony for Southern Claims Commission, No. 5225, April 22, 1876.

97 Voluntary statement of Dr. George B. Peters, Annals of the Army of the Cumberland," 1864, p. 618.

Dr. Peters plantation home north of Marianna, AR where he stayed a year before returning to Spring Hill. Photo in possession of Rosemary Harper. Butch Harper was a great grandson of Jessie and Dr. Peters.

General Earl "Buck" Van Dorn

Earl Van Dorn was born on September 17, 1820, near Port Gibson, Mississippi, the fourth of nine children of Peter Aaron and Sofia Donelson Caffery Van Dorn. His father claimed Holland ancestry whose father was Lord High Chancellor to the King. The family came to America in the early seventeenth century and bought lands from the Indians in the area of New Jersey. His parents felt that Peter was more interested in books than the farm, and sent him to Princeton College to be a preacher. At the age of twenty-one, he announced that he could preach but not pray and made his way to the territory of Mississippi. He studied law, received a life appointment as Judge of the Orphans' Court for the southern district, and made his home in Port Gibson. His wife Sophie was the niece of Rachel Donelson, who married President Andrew Jackson.

Sophie and her three oldest daughters would dote on the flaxen haired, bright steel blue eyed Earl. When he was ten, his mother died and his two older sisters had married leaving fourteen year old Octavia to care for everyone. Judge Van Dorn sent Earl and his brother Aaron, who was two years younger, to an academy in Maryland where he thought that they would receive a better education.[98]

---

98 Emily Van Dorn Miller, *A Soldier's Honor With Reminiscences of Major-General Earl Van Dorn,* (New York: The Abbey Press, 1902), p. 14-18.

Earl returned to Port Gibson and entered Oakland College about eighteen miles away in 1837 only seven years after it was established under the Mississippi Presbytery.[99] When it opened as a simple grammar school with three pupils, there were sixty-five by the end of the session. The principal object of Oakland College was to educate young men for the ministry.[100] At the age of sixteen, Earl wrote a letter to his great uncle President Andrew Jackson at the Hermitage asking for an appointment to West Point. Earl was in Baltimore where he was feeling dejected and depressed, but he finally got his commission after several months.[101] His brother-in-law John Vertner wrote a letter to the Honorable R. I. Walker asking that his ward Earl Van Dorn and the son of his old acquaintance Judge Van Dorn be given an appointment because a vacancy existed in Mississippi to enter West Point. Although a recommendation was mentioned in the correspondence from General Jackson, permission to be a cadet had to be obtained from Vertner."[102]

Apparently, Earl was not considering the will left by his father that was recorded in March of 1837 that stated his desire for Earl and Aaron to be educated at the National College in the City of Washington. As soon as they qualified to enter, they were to continue there for four years, and after graduation, remain in Washington to study the profession that they choose.[103]

The will also stated that the two youngest children, Emily and Jacob, would be in the care of two of their sisters and their husbands. Mary, who was the wife of John C. Lacey, and Jane, who was the

---

99 O. Sulivane letter to her sister Jane from Murray J. Smith collection, U. S. Military History Institute, Carlisle Barracks, PA. Annotations to letter July 12-16, 1992 by Edgar Crisler (deceased), Port Gibson, MS who located the letter.

100 "Biographical and Historical Memoirs of Mississippi, (Chicago: Goodspeed Publishing Company 1891)

101 *Op. Cit., Miller*

102 Earl Van Dorn file at U. S. Military Academy, West Point, Letter from J. W. Vertner to R. I. Walker dated April 28, 1838.

103 Will recorded in Claiborne County, Mississippi, 1837, Peter A Vandorn, Book A, pp. 346-348.

wife of John D. Vertner were to have the care and management although John's father Daniel was appointed sole executor with unlimited power at his discretion.[104] It was stated in the family history that the brothers filed suit seeking an accounting of his management of their father's estate. It was filed after Earl entered West Point and handled by Hugh Short, the husband of a first cousin. Vertner died before the estate was settled.[105]

Although Aaron was just two years younger than Earl, he is seldom mentioned. The sisters were very attentive to the first brother and apparently Aaron led quite a different life. As Earl had done, he attended Oakland College but for one year beginning in 1839.[106] It is not known what he did until he is working in California. He is listed as a deputy surveyor on a Napa County map that was commissioned to survey Rancho Las Putas in the months of November and December 1852. The survey was issued in an order by the Board of United States Commissioners "to ascertain aid better private land claims for California." It was dated San Francisco, California, 2nd July 1852, and "in conformity with a letter of authorization and instruction from the U.S. Surveyor General of Public Lands for the state of California dated San Francisco, Cal., Oct. 20, 1852 containers a commission to survey the Rancho de Las Putas Maria Anastasia Higuera de Berreyesa etat tamento on Putas River in Napa County, California.[107]

Aaron testified in a U. S. District Court trial as Deputy U. S. Surveyor concerning a grant in 1855 and grant patents to Maria Antonia Mesa in 1872.

Margaret Vertner Leonard, a niece of Aaron and Earl, wrote that Aaron was a civil engineer. He was selected by the United States Government to join Col. John Fremont, the Great Pathfinder, who was known for his surveying expeditions and Senator William

---

104 *Ibid.*
105 *Op. Cit., O. Sulivane*
106 *Ibid.*
107 Map in Bancroft Library, University of California, Berkeley, California.

Guinn to survey the Pacific Coast. Guin of California had been the personal secretary of Andrew Jackson in 1831 and no doubt was aware of the Van Dorns. He lived for a time in Clinton, Mississippi located west of Jackson and not too far from Port Gibson. As a resident of California, he knew John C. Fremont, who also became a senator. Guin was able to get $40,000 for a survey of the Pacific Coast during his second term that was 1857-1861. Aaron's notes were used for drawing the maps and were referred to as a "work of art." They were displayed in one of the departments for several years.[108]

Aaron was involved in the early history of Death Valley as a cartographer of the actual official maps of the bleak region of the country drawn by him in 1857. He went along with an Army expedition in the area specifically for the purpose of mapping the region. His originals are in the National Archives.[109] In 1860 he is living in San Francisco with his sister Jane Vertner age 45 and her daughter 27. Both of them were widows by this time and could have gone there because of the impending unrest in the country.[110] Jane had a son also named Aaron, who would lose his life in the Battle of Shiloh two years later.[111]

Aaron continued to survey and draw maps. The first published map that named Death Valley was Farley's mining district map of 1861. But he used an unpolished map that was drawn by Aaron Van Dorn in 1861 who was assistant surveyor for the United States.[112]

In 1861 the U. S. Congress ordered a reconnaissance of California's eastern boundary in preparation for a survey of that boundary. It was to begin in Amargosa Valley, but because of poor water, grass, and old mules, the reconnaissance party crossed Death Valley and ascended the Panamint Range toward Townes Pass. Dr.

---

108 Letter from Margaret Vertner Leonard, niece to Earl Van Dorn, to her cousin Vera Morel.
109 *Op. cit,.* O. Sulivane letter.
110 1860 Census, San Francisco, CA.
111 *Op. Cit., O. Sulivane Letter.*
112 William Lewis Manley, Leroy C. Johnson, and Jean Johnson, *Escape from Death Valley*, (Science: 1987), p., 23.

J. R. N. Owen, who was a physician and miner and had mining claims in the southern Casa Mountains, led the group with Aaron as assistant surveyor for the boundary commission and topographer for the reconnaissance who became the unofficial recorder.[113]

Aaron wrote "Eastern Boundary Sketches" in the 1861 edition of the Sacramento *Daily Union* that contained an account and expedition. He is the only one not named besides a camel driver; but it is obvious that he composed the articles because of the professional references and exact incidences where he identified Dr. Owen.[114] Camels had been introduced in the desert areas by Jefferson Davis when he was Secretary of War in the 1850s. The camel's dromedary feet were excellent for the sand but became bruised in the rocky areas. With the beginning of the War, this objective was soon forgotten.[115]

It was recorded in the *Sacramento Bee* of March 15, 1869 that Aaron Van Dorn died on the twelfth at the age of 45. For some reason, his death was recorded in other places occurring five years later. By the 1870 census, he is not listed, but his sister and her daughter are located in Port Gibson, Mississippi; however, his sister dies the same year. He was of a very calm and quiet disposition, very reserved and avoided people and social engagements. He liked to read and led a very secluded life but was always pleasant to the children of his relatives.[116]

It was stated that in the family history that Aaron was rather mysterious having never married, lived apart from the family, and

---

113 LeRoy Johnson and Jean Johnson, "Where is Van Dorn's 'Hitchins Spring,'" from Proceedings Third Death Valley Conference on History, January 30-February 6, 1992, Death Valley, CA, Death Valley Natural History Association, p. 45-56.

114 One of the Exploring Party of the last US Boundary Commission (Aaron Van Dorn) "Eastern Boundary Commission," Sacramento Daily Union, Number IV, July 11, 1861.

115 Jefferson Davis, Secretary of War, Report to the President, December 4, 1854, p. 8.

116 *Op. Cit.*, Letter from Margaret Vertner Leonard.

communicated little. In *A Soldier's Honor with Reminiscences of Major-General Earl Van Dorn* by his sister Emily Van Dorn Miller, she does not mention anything about his life except when he and Earl were sent to school in Maryland.

As soon as Earl received his commission, he packed his bags and immediately traveled to West Point where he stayed for four years without returning home. He had become depressed over not hearing from any appointment and thought that he would never hear from his request.[117] His record indicates that he was number 211 of 1838 received. It is obvious that being recommended by Andrew Jackson exerted a great deal of influence for Earl's being accepted. His record was nothing to be proud with 183 demerits in his last year just short of a dismissal at 200. He was guilty of failing to salute in passing, smoking tobacco in quarters, not attending church, and failing to suppress profanity of his friends. His uniform was constantly out of order, shoes not blackened, late, not being present at all, or visiting. His best grades were in art class, and his talent is evident in the art that he completed throughout the years.[118]

Earl related a story to his niece about seeing Fanny Elssler, a famous Austrian ballerina, while he was a cadet. She was performing in a benefit to raise funds for the Bunker Hill monument. A Group of prominent citizens including Daniel Webster organized the Bunker Hill Monument Association to construct a permanent and noteworthy monument to commemorate the first major battle of the Revolutionary War.[119] Fanny came to the United States in 1840 and was known to have been escorted and dined by John Van Buren, son of the President, but after two years returned to Europe.[120] Earl asked for a leave and "made a bee line" to pay $3.00 for the performance. He obtained a seat in the pit in front of the footlights

---

117 *Op. Cit.*, Emily Van Dorn Miller.
118 Earl Van Dorn file at U. S. Military Academy, West Point, Order of General Merit p. 12; Delinquencies p. 280, 1941-1942.
119 Charlestown, MA, Bunker Hill, Boston National Historical Park.
120 Ivor Forbes Guest, *Fanny Elssler*, (Connecticut: Wesleyan University Press 1970), p. 134.

that was full of bald heads and no women. An elderly toothless Quaker moved quietly and took the seat next to him. Fanny set in motion as she came bouncing in on tip toe, began whirling, twirling, and kicked too high for the Quaker's modesty. He turned to Earl and commented, "This is no fitting place for thee and me, young man." However, the Quaker continued to sit in his seat until the final performance.[121]

Earl finally brought his grades up to graduate number 52nd while his friend James Longstreet graduated number 54th out of 56 in the West Point Class of 1842. There were several distinguished members of the class who also fought for the Confederacy in addition to the Mexican-American War as Earl.[122]

Among them were Gustavus W. Smith who was only 16 when he entered but graduated 8th; Mansfield Lovell who was only 15 but graduated 9th; Daniel H. Hill who was the brother-in-law of Stonewall Jackson; and Alexander P. Stewart who graduated 12th and became a teacher at Cumberland University in Lebanon, Tennessee. Among Union generals were William Rosecrans who graduated 5th; Abner Doubleday who graduated 24th with 132 demerits, but is known more for developing baseball. Very few are aware that Doubleday obtained a patent for the cable car railway in San Francisco that still runs today.[123] U. S. Grant graduated 20th out of 41 in the following class with 98 demerits.[124]

Assigned first as an infantry lieutenant in the Seventh Infantry Regiment at Fort Pike, Louisiana on the Gulf of Mexico, Earl's low grades left him no choice that September after graduation. In December he was transferred to Alabama where his service

---

121 *Op. Cit.*, Letter from Margaret Vertner Leonard.
122 *Op. Cit.*, Order of General Merit p. 12; Delinquencies p. 280, 1941-1942.
123 N. Sanford Ramey, *Triumphs of Genius*, (Philadelphia: A. R. Keller 1893), p. 272.
124 *Op. Cit.*

alternated for two years between Fort Morgan and Mount Vernon Arsenal.[125]

Earl Van Dorn known as "Buck" was described as handsome, having regular features on his less than five feet eight frame, fine blue eyes, and wavy blond hair. He had a superior physique and poise and was an excellent horseman. It was obvious that he was a lady's man. While stationed at Mount Vernon Arsenal, he met Caroline Godbold, the daughter of a prominent resident in the area. His sister Emily described Carrie as a girlish looking little woman, modest and shy, slight, and graceful.

They had a whirlwind courtship and married a few months later when she was only sixteen. Her parents did not approve, and when Earl was sent on his assignment away from Alabama, her parents insisted that she stay and not go with him.[126]

Earl and Carrie's (He refers to her as Carry in his letters.) separations were often and for long periods of time. This was probably the cause of Earl's getting involved with Martha Goodbread of Texas. She followed him as a laundress at the fort frequently under the name of Smith. Martha had a son she called Percy in 1857 in Texas, a daughter Lammie Belle born in Kansas on October 1, 1859, and another son in Arkansas whom she named Douglas on November 1, 1861. The children always went by the name of Van Dorn, but Martha went by Goodbread or Smith.[127]

Martha was born in Green County, Alabama, in 1836 about 200 miles north of Mt. Vernon, the home of Caroline Van Dorn. When her parents migrated to Texas, she apparently did not accompany them with her older and younger sisters. She may have had a job as a laundress with the 2nd Cavalry with the intent to join her family later when they went to Ft. Mason the following year, but some accounts

---

125 *Op. Cit., Miller*, p. 19.
126 Arthur B. Carter, *The Tarnished Cavalier*, (Knoxville: The University of Tennessee Press, 1999), 3-5.
127 Barbara Cope, Great Granddaughter of Earl Van Dorn and Martha Goodbread, Dallas, Texas, Goodbread and Van Dorn papers in personal collection, Interview 2010.

believe that she refused to a go along with them. Each time that she had a child, Earl Van Dorn was located in the same area.[128]

Earl fought in the Mexican War under Zachary Taylor and fellow officers included: Jefferson Davis, George B. McClellan, George B. Meade, Robert E. Lee, Ulysses S. Grant, P. G. T. Beauregard, and Braxton Bragg. He fought in the taking of Vera Cruz, Chapultepec, and Mexico City where he was wounded in the foot. Earl enlightened among the stories that he told while he was there concerned the very beautiful Mexican women and their fan flirtations. Every turn or movement of the fan held a particular significance with the opening and shutting of the fan being a genuine challenge.[129]

After the occupation in Mexico City ended, Earl served in Florida, Kentucky, Louisiana, Mississippi, and fighting Comanche Indians in Texas. He returned home after four years to find that his children scarcely knew who he was. Earl took Carrie and his niece Margaret on a trip to Mobile aboard the *Robert Ward* that was a glorious boat of comfort and luxury. Margaret related in later years that their seats were at the captain's table and included champagne, feast of good things, a flow of character and humor, toasts and anecdotes were exchanged. They were in New Orleans four days after they boarded the steamer in Natchez. Staying in the Battle House in Mobile that was described as a delightful rendezvous for the officers of the army, the group met Judah P. Benjamin. He had been in the Louisiana House of Representatives and a United States Senator but would be remembered as the only Jewish representative of three departments of the Confederacy having served as Attorney General, Secretary of War, and Secretary of State.[130]

On that evening, they attended the theater to see John Wilkes Booth and Fanny Davenport who had been billed for that night a month before. Booth was a magnet who knew his audiences and drew enormous houses. That night, the house was packed full with no standing room but fortunately, the group had reservations. When

---

128 *Ibid.*
129 *Op. Cit.*, Letter from Margaret Vertner Leonard.
130 *Ibid.*

General Pierre Beauregard and Major Earl Van Dorn in full military dress approached the area, a shout and three cheers for the Army arose. The curtain slowly went up as a breathless expectancy and a remarkable silence swept those in attendance. Booth cautiously entered the stage when wild and jubilant emotion vibrated from the house. He stood one instant, bowed before his admirers, and then became Hamlet. He was superb as he played upon the pulses of that overcrowded room as no other actor of his time. Fanny Davenport was less than ten years old when she performed that night, but she continued to become a well known actress for forty more years.[131]

On February 3, 1860, the Mississippi Legislature was in session in Jackson and passed a resolution in relation to the presentation of a sword to Major Earl Van Dorn of the United States Army. It stated:

> ...desirous to testify its appreciation of the services of a citizen, whose conduct has entitled him to an expression of public approbation—request the Governor to cause to be prepared and be presented to Major Earl Van Dorn, of the United States Army, a sword, suitable to express the high esteem in which he is held by his native State, for the gallantry he has shown in the many battles he has fought for his country.

By the middle of May 1861, the governor asked that an inscription be placed on the sword that read: "Presented to Major Earl Van Dorn by the State of Mississippi in testimony of her appreciation of the gallantry of her native son, in many battles." On the other side was to be the inscription: "By order of the State of Mississippi, February 3, 1860."

After Lincoln's election in November 1860, there was a great deal of talk concerning succession. By December, South Carolina held a state convention that voted to secede from the union. Earl went to Mobile, Alabama, by boat, and Carrie met him there. On January 3, 1861, Earl Van Dorn severed his connections with

---

131 *Ibid.*

the army where he had served with distinction as an officer for eighteen years. By January 9, Mississippi joined the secession, and Earl offered his services. By February he became a member of the first volunteers, and when the State Convention elected Jefferson Davis its major general of state troops, Earl became the chief of the brigadiers assigned to Davis' staff.[132] By February 4, Jefferson Davis was elected Provisional President of the Confederate States of America during the convention of the Provisional Congress that was held in Montgomery, Alabama.

Others soon followed and by April 12, 1861, the war officially began with the attack on Ft. Sumter. "I am now in for it," Van Dorn wrote his wife, "to make a reputation and serve my country conspicuously or fail. I must not, shall not, do the latter."

Although Van Dorn entered the Confederate army as a colonel, he was sent soon after the War started by President Jefferson Davis to Texas where with a few men captured the Federal steamer *Star of the West* that had come to evacuate Federal troops. They surrendered their weapons, and those who did not join the Confederates were paroled. The ship later became a receiving vessel in the Confederate Navy.[133] Van Dorn received a promotion to brigadier general and soon another to major general. His was a star quickly on the rise, and in January of 1862, it burned yet brighter when Davis gave him command of the Trans-Mississippi District Department 2. [134]

General Albert S. Johnston called upon Van Dorn to join the Army of Tennessee in Corinth, Mississippi, to keep the Union army from advancing. In spite of this, Van Dorn was selected to be sent to defend Arkansas from Brig. Gen. Samuel Curtis' Union invasion. The Confederate troops included General Price's Missouri state guards, General McCulloch's division, and General Pike's three regiments of Choctaw Indians. On March 7, 1862, Van Dorn

---

132 Robert G. Hartje, *The Life and Times of a Confederate General*, (Nashville: Vanderbilt University Press, 1967), 76-77.
133 *Op. Cit., Miller*, p. 300-303.
134 Anne J. Bailey, *Encyclopedia of the Confederacy*, (New York: Simon & Schuster 1993), pp. 1661-1662.

and Gen. Sterling Price collided with Union forces on a high peak near Elk Horn Tavern at Pea Ridge. Although outnumbering their enemy, they had weak communication, mismanaged strategy, and divided forces causing the loss of the ammunition train. Van Dorn endured heavy losses and personally had chills and fever brought on by his boat capsizing while crossing an icy river. Much of his time was spent in an ambulance. He immediately received orders to bring his army to Corinth, Mississippi, but arrived too late to participate in the Battle of Shiloh near Savannah, Tennessee.[135]

Always criticized for his methods, Van Dorn had a commendable defense of Vicksburg, Mississippi, in June followed by a disastrous defeat in Corinth, Mississippi. Attacking his old West Point classmate, Maj. Gen. William S. Rosecrans, in October at Corinth proved disastrous for his career as well as his army. His failed frontal assaults against the fortifications he himself had built when previously at Corinth resulted in a court of inquiry charging him with negligence that questioned Van Dorn's conduct in the battle.[136]

Jefferson Davis had been fond of Earl Van Dorn and had no doubt been an influence in the promotion of his career. After the battle at Corinth, Van Dorn was ruthlessly criticized for his loss. General John S. Bowen charged him with "cruel and improper treatment of officers and soldiers under his command." It was widely rumored that he was drunk during the battle. Van Dorn wrote President Davis to grant him a trial so he would have a chance to clear his name; in spite of this, Davis ordered a court of inquiry.[137]

When the court of inquiry convened at Abbeville on November 15, 1862, it consisted of Generals Sterling Price, Dabney Maury, and Lloyd Tilghman. It was obvious that it was weighed towards Van Dorn. General Price had been with him during the battle at

---

135 William L. Shea and Earl J. Hess, *Pea Ridge: Civil War Campaign in the West,* (Chapel Hill: The University of North Carolina Press 1992), pp. 55-61.
136 *Op. Cit.,* Arthur R. Carter, pp. 116-117.
137 *Ibid., p. 118.*

Pea Ridge and Corinth. General Maury, the nephew of Matthew Fontaine Maury with whom he lived since he was two years old, was Van Dorn's Chief of Staff. General Tilghman had been in the Mexican War as well as Van Dorn and a graduate of West Point; however, he came from a military family and was known for obeying the rules and going by the book.[138]

In his opening statement, Van Dorn declared: "I desire to call your attention to these facts—that I have been a soldier for nearly a quarter of a century—that this is the first time that I have been called upon to defend myself against allegations of any kind; though my career has been an eventful one—that I have accumulated nothing of the world's wealth, having devoted my whole time and energies to the service of my country; therefore, my reputation is all that belongs to me without which life to me were as valueless as the crisp and faded leaf of autumn."[139] He was actually court-martialed for his role but was found not guilty although remained under suspicion by some of his fellow officers. The court acquitted him of the charges that included neglect of duty and cruel and improper treatment of officers and soldiers under his command. On the other hand, he was now under the close supervision of Lt. Gen. John C. Pemberton, who placed him in charge of his cavalry forces at Vicksburg. It was also reported that every one of the men in the court of inquiry wept with the decision along with others in the room. The only one who did not was Van Dorn who was described by his attorney as, "To him it was not a matter of tears, but as one of principle, existence, life, honor, emphatically 'to be or not to be.'"[140]

In Jefferson Davis' Papers, there is a letter from Van Dorn written from Grenada, Mississippi, on December 8, 1862, to John S. Bowen:

Dear General
    I am enabled to send you the action of the Court of

---

138 *Ibid., p. 117.*
139 *Op. Cit.,* Emily Van Dorn Miller, p. 158.
140 *Ibid.,* p. 230.

Inquiry in my case—I also send you my written defense, which I hope you will do me the kindness to read, as it covers nearly the whole ground of the accusations—You will see that every charge has been disproved—

I have heard from several sources that it has been reported to you that I was a Seducer and a libertine—that I had seduced the daughter of a respectable citizen of Vicksburg etc, etc. The nature of such charges prevents investigation—but as a Christian and before my God I do most solemnly declare that it is false—that I not only did not seduce the young lady referred to but that I sever seduced any young lady in my life—and further that, with the exception of my wife, I have never had intercourse with any woman, as I believe, who was not alike accessible to others—there was a wild frolicksome young lady of Vicksburg whose acquaintance I made during the defense, whose indiscretions as well, probably as some of my own, may have given grounds for the prudish and censorious to slander, and the idle talk, but that young lady, I believe to be as virtuous as any young lady in Vicksburg or in Miss—She has been most shamefully punished for hers, as I have been for my thoughtlessness and folly—or pleasantries as they may be called--...........

I am sorry to call your attention so much to personal matters, but "from the fullness of the heart the mouth speaketh," and I feel very deeply my present position—

> Very truly & respectfully
> Sir I am your friend & Obt. Sevt
> Earl Van Dorn
> Majr. Genl

General Bowen would die of dysentery while near Vicksburg, Mississippi, two months after the death of Van Dorn. Tilghman would die in battle nine days after Van Dorn. Price became so thoroughly disgusted with Van Dorn's promotion after Pea Ridge that he went to see President Davis to discuss his grievances and get permission to return to Missouri only to have Davis question his loyalty. He referred to Price as the "vainest man I ever met. Maury described Van Dorn as ..."his bright face lighted with kindliness and courage, we all loved to see him. His figure was lithe and graceful; his stature did not exceed five feet six inches; but his clear blue eyes, his firm-set mouth, with white, strong teeth, his well-cut nose, with expanding nostrils, gave assurance of a man whom men could trust and follow. There was no self-seeking in him, and he would die for duty at any moment. His personal traits were very charming. His person was very handsome; his manners frank and simple; with his friends he was genial and sometimes convivial; but never did I know him to postpone his duty for pleasure, or to pursue conviviality to a degree unbecoming a gentleman. Take him for all in all he was the most gallant soldier I have ever known."[141]

Van Dorn was able to regain his reputation when he defeated General Grant at Holly Springs, Mississippi, in December. He had a raid on Grant's supply base that was captured or destroyed that was valued $400,000 to $1,500,000. Van Dorn was aggressive although at times reckless but was suited for the cavalry.[142] He had finally found his mission when he joined the successful General Nathan Bedford Forrest's cavalry in Tennessee. In early 1863, he was able to prove his military expertise by his extraordinary success at Thompson's Station the first of March. He and Forrest had their own battle over disposition of supplies captured by Forrest, and Van Dorn's accusation that Forrest had claimed a victory at Thompson Station north of Spring Hill. The dispute was settled when Forrest said, "I have enough Yankees to fight without fighting you."[143]

Earl's sister Octavia lived in Belvoir, Maryland, but had been visiting in Port Gibson during December. She wrote her sister Jane, who was in San Francisco with her daughter Margaret and staying with their brother Aaron. She wrote about the charges

---

141 Major-General Dabney H. Maury, *Southern Historical Society Papers*, Volume 19. Reverend J. William Jones, Ed.

142 Clay Williams, "Holly Springs Raid," *Encyclopedia of the American Civil War: A Political, Social, and Military History*,(Santa Barbara: ABC-CLIO 2000), pp. 986-987.

143 John Allan Wyeth, *Life of General Nathan Bedford Forrest*, (New York: Harper & Brothers Publishers 1899), p. 176-177.

that were brought against General Van Dorn in Corinth and the drunkenness affecting his character as an officer. He was cleared of all charges, and Octavia mentions, "Of course that is all false about his having left his wife or of her suing for a divorce from him. I do not know whether he had heard the report or not, he did not mention it, but told me he had received a letter from Caroline a few days before..."[144]

It is not known if General Van Dorn had any more contact with Martha Goodbread. Their third child, Douglas, was born on November 1, 1861, in Arkansas while Van Dorn was commanding the 1st Division, Potomac District, Department of Northern Virginia from October 22 to January 10, 1862. The only opportunity he may have seen her would have been while he was in Pea Ridge, Arkansas, in March.

General Van Dorn and his troops arrived in Columbia, Tennessee, in February 1863 and immediately received the attention of many captivated ladies who spoke of his handsomeness and gallantry. There were some raids and skirmishes during this time, but after a month, a large stable on the northeast corner of South Main and Eighth Streets caught fire. It was a long-one-story house with a basement being used as stables with a large amount of hay and feed. About 2:00 am, a fire broke out and spread rapidly. Most of Van Dorn's staff and escort had their very first-rate horses in this location. One officer pressed through the smoke and brought his fine bay horse to the front door, but no amount of urging or driving could get the horse out. He stood there a moment and then broke into the flames behind him.

The screaming of the horses would never be forgotten by those who heard it. Only a few were saved, and the escort alone lost 65. Because of the closeness of the other houses, the carcasses could not be drenched with oil and burned. They were hauled to the east of town, and then the scraps were removed. It took several days that were rather warm and no disinfectants were available. It

---

144 *Op. Cit.*, Letter.

was a most difficult situation that was completed by Major Amos W. Warfield, acting as Post Quartermaster. It was suspected that a paroled Federal prisoner and possible wounded Federal soldiers in the hospital that was located in the Columbia Female Academy about four blocks away on West Seventh were the culprits.

Years after the war, a Columbia woman on her death bed admitted that a Maury County Union man had confessed to her in confidence. He had fired the stable so as to destroy the horses of Van Dorn, the staff, and escort. As he moved north quite soon after and had died recently, leaving relatives in Columbia, she refrained from mentioning his name.[145]

General Van Dorn moved to Spring Hill shortly after the incident and established his headquarters in the home of Dr. and Mrs. Aaron White on Duplex Road just off the main route near the downtown area.

The forty-one year old Dr. White could not join the Confederate Army because of his deafness but supported the South throughout the War as a physician and surgeon. He had construction begun on the Greek Revival house in 1844 while he practiced medicine in Spring Hill and the Jackson College area, and it was completed by his brother Henry within the year and christened "White Hall." It was nothing unusual for Dr. White to take in critically sick patients in his home and be with them until they recovered or go into a patient's home and stay until they were improved. When General Van Dorn, his staff, and aides-de-camp moved into White Hall, Dr. and Mrs. White and his family of two small children were left the kitchen wing and one bedroom. [146]

Many of the men who rode with Van Dorn admired him and would protect him whenever necessary knowing full well his reputation with women and liquor. Others tolerated his actions,

---

[145] Frank A. Smith, *History of Maury County, Tennessee,* compiled by Maury County Historical Society. 1969. pp. 117-118.

[146] Jill Garrett, "The Ghost Rides at White Hall-White Hall Added to the National Register," *Columbia Daily Herald*, June 1973.

but when it spilled over into the general population, it was difficult to ignore.

William, known as Will, L. Biggers was the oldest of ten children of Andrew Jackson C. and Malinda Hartley Biggers. He was twenty when the War started, and he and his brother Lum, who was two years younger, joined the Confederate Army. He was soon discharged in the fall while he was in Bowling Green, Kentucky, for "palpitation of the heart." It was stated that later he was to join Forrest's forces or with General Van Dorn's Cavalry. While Will was home on sick leave, he decided to go to Franklin and visit another brother who joined the Union and was serving with Stokes Federal Cavalry. Shortly after his visit, eight of Van Dorn's men stationed at nearby Spring Hill went to the Biggers' home. They pulled Will from his home, took him to Pulltight Hill, and shot him five times in the stomach. They took his horse and saddle and left him for dead. When Lum heard of his brother's death, he hurried home and then later went to Van Dorn's headquarters. When he entered the camp, he saw Will's horse and saddle and immediately went to Van Dorn with the information and the good recommendation that he had received from Pat Cleburne, Hardee, and Bragg. Van Dorn's rude treatment of Lum so enraged him to the extent that Lum went into the Federal lines and joined the Union forces under Colonel William B. Stokes. The community became divided after Will's murder, and an entire company of soldiers was raised to join the Union Army although the community was almost entirely Confederate sympathizers. The murder was so senseless and brutal that residents believe that Will's spirit still haunts Pulltight Hill.[147]

---

147 Louise G. Lynch, *Flat Creek Its Land and its People* Ancestor information in possession of LaDelle Smith, Lewisburg, Tennessee.

General Van Dorn and Jessie Peters

General Van Dorn was again getting all the attention and glorification from ladies in the Spring Hill area. In his dazzling uniform, tall, erect, handsome, with bright flashing eyes, cameo-like features, and a graceful, well-proportioned form, he had that winning charm of manner and personal magnetism so persuasive in love and friendship. He was described as familiar with classical and modern literature, an unique storyteller, with an inexhaustible supply of quotations; he was a delightful fireside and table companion, as welcome in the politest society as in camps and bivouac. During a long, active, eventful career, he never lost a friend or justly made an enemy.

He attended several activities, and he had military reviews that were very festive and invited all the ladies. A trooper complained that the cavalry wasted its time in reviews and dress parades "for a few lonesome and garish young ladies."[148] Van Dorn and several of his officers were seen in the company of Jessie in her carriage. In a letter of a student attending the Columbia Athenaeum, she mentioned that

> Clara Peters and her roommates, two pretty girls from Kentucky, were the "big girls;" and they let me keep my dolls in their room and come there to play sometimes.

---

148 *Op. Cit.*, Garrett.

One Friday afternoon we little girls were all agog when Clara's stepmother, young Mrs. Peters, who lived in Spring Hill, came to take Clara and her roommates home for the weekend. What excited out interest and curiosity was the style in which Mrs. Peters came—several soldiers in uniform on prancing horses as out-riders. In the carriage as her escort was the dashing Confederate general who had so lately distinguished himself in Mississippi, the very handsome, ideal West Pointer, General Earl Van Dorn. We watched them all drive off laughing and happy. Next day the girls were brought back to the school, sad and shaken by the terrible tragedy they had witnessed. For that night, Mr. Peters returned unexpectedly from a trip and, finding the general in his wife's bed, shot and killed him.[149]

The middle of April, Jessie Peters made a morning visit to White Hall, the home of Dr. and Mrs. White, and the current headquarters of General Van Dorn. Dressed in a stylish black velvet riding habit and a matching hat embellished with large black ostrich plumes, she courteously requested to see the general. Mrs. White graciously welcomed and invited Jessie to come in and be seated in the parlor while she informed the general who was upstairs in the northeast room that there was someone to see him. Jessie wanted to see the General privately and at once. About the time that Mrs. White started to the second floor, Jessie haughtily swept past, "Do not bother, Mrs. White. I'll run up there and see him." She lingered for an hour, and when the scene was repeated three days later, Mrs. White was determined that this inappropriateness would not continue in her home. When Dr. White arrived home, she demanded, "You must get the General out of this house. You know Mrs. Peters. There is going to be trouble between Dr. Peters and the General. It must not happen here."

Dr. White felt an awkwardness in approaching the problem, but when he went to the General, he diplomatically called to the

---

[149] Mary Gordon Stimson, *A Long Remembrance*, Diane Stimson Webb, Waunakee, WI, 1988, p. 36.

General's attention to the fact that Mrs. White was in ill health, how his family was so crowded with two small children, and if possible, to find other headquarters. The General and his staff occupied all of the house except one bedroom and the kitchen. Van Dorn was very courteous and said that he had noticed the crowded conditions, and he would be looking for more spacious quarters and expected to leave in a few days.[150]

In a day or so later, Van Dorn informed the Whites that he would be moving to the home of Martin Cheairs, the brother of Nathaniel, who was married to Jessie's sister Susan. The back of Jessie's house could be seen from this location although it was facing another road.

Dr. Peters had been at his property in Arkansas below Memphis for about a year when on April 4, he returned to Memphis to get a pass to leave the Federal lines. He crossed the rebel lines at the Tennessee River.[151] He arrived at Spring Hill on the 12th and was immediately distressed at the scandalized rumors that General Van Dorn had been extremely attentive to Jessie. Although he was alarmed at the distressing rumors that flourished in the community, he continued to doubt as to the guilt of Jessie. The incidents of guilt began to mount even to the extent that a servant came to the Peters' house to deliver a note from the General. Dr. Peters glared at him when he said emphatically, "I will blow your brains out if I ever see you enter these premises again, and you tell that whiskey-headed master, General Van Dorn, that I will blow his brains out as well, or any of his staff that step their foot inside of this lawn."[152]

On the 22nd Dr. Peters went to Nashville and learned when he

---

150 J. R. Peacock interview with granddaughter of Dr. Aaron White, March 24, 1951.
151 U. S. National Archives & Records Administration, RG 123, Cong. #3690, George B. Peters Testimony for Southern Claims Commission, No. 5225, April 22, 1876.
152 *Annals of the Army of the Cumberland*, Voluntary statement of Dr. George B. Peters to army police in Nashville, Tennessee, 1864, p. 618-620.

returned that Van Dorn had been at the Peters' house every night while he was gone with no one with her except their small children. Determined to catch the General, Dr. Peters pretended a trip to Shelbyville but actually did not leave the premises. The second night about 2:30 in the morning after his supposed absence, he went into the house and found Van Dorn with Jessie. The General acknowledged that Dr. Peters had every right to kill him, but he would exonerate Jessie from dishonor and incriminate himself completely. He agreed to make certain acknowledgements over his own signature, and with this, Dr. Peters agreed to give his life to his wife and children. The General accepted the proposition upon the honor of a soldier but stated that he cared very little for his wife. Dr. Peters ordered him off the grounds about 3:00.[153]

The next day Dr. Peters was too sick to go see the General, but early the next morning, he mounted his horse and made his way from his house to the downtown area of Spring Hill. It was about 8:00 when Dr. Peters made his way to the Martin Cheairs' home and entered the General's office room waiting to receive the written confession.[154]

On the morning of May 7, Van Dorn rose from the breakfast table alone in advance of his staff to go to his office headquarters in the southeast section on the first floor of the Cheairs' home.[155] When he arrived, Dr. Peters was already there waiting for him. Attempting to evade the situation, the General started a conversation as to its appropriateness. Dr. Peters was not pleased when the papers that he requested were not prepared, and he gave Van Dorn half an hour to complete them and told him that he knew the consequences if he refused to comply.[156]

Dr. Peters left and went into Spring Hill to discuss with a friend the current circumstances of the situation. As he rode down the

---

153 *Ibid.*
154 *Ibid.*
155 A. W. Sparks, *The War Between the States as I Saw It*, Victor M. Rose interview, (Tyler: Lee & Burnett, Publishers 1901), p. 107.
156 *Op. Cit.*, Voluntary statement.

street trying to light his pipe, he saw F. K. Odil walking up the street. He rode over and asked him for a light. A rather scarce article at the time, Odel went into a nearby cobbler's shop to get a coal of fire on a chip of wood.[157]

Fountain Kerr Odil was a small man who was not very tall. He was described as an "example of what Christian people should be." With goodness and kindness, life was not easy with eleven children, but he did not depart from his Presbyterian beliefs. Going to church was a must in his household, and before going to bed, there was family prayer and reading of the Bible each night. His motto was, and he held to it, "Never spend a dollar until you have made it."[158]

After lighting his pipe, Dr. Peters turned his horse and started down toward Van Dorn's headquarters. Odil had some business to transact with Martin Cheairs and started walking in the same direction when he saw Dr. Peters enter the house.[159] Sol Gregory, a courier, was in the office and had just been given a dispatch to be carried to General Nathan Bedford Forrest, who was located sixteen miles south of the Tennessee River.[160]

Entering the office room, Dr. Peters found Van Dorn writing at his desk. He read what he had written, and he agreed that it was written in accordance with what they had agreed; however, the second part was a misrepresentation and a lie. Van Dorn refused to comply with what they had agreed because it would injure the cause, the service, and his reputation if it were made public. Dr. Peters was incensed at his reply, "You did not think so thirty hours ago when your life was in my hands. You were then ready

---

157 William Ewing Fowler, *Stories and Legends of Maury County, Tennessee*, Interview of F. K. Odil, Graduate School of Education, George Peabody School for Teachers, June 1937, p. 188.
158 *Columbia Daily Herald*, Columbia, Tennessee, May 8, 1916. 60th Wedding Anniversary.
159 William Ewing Fowler, *Stories & Legends of Maury County Tennessee*, Dept. of English Graduate School of Education, George Peabody College for Teachers, June 1937, p. 188.
160 Interview with John Solomon Repps Gregory, November 4, 1903.

to promise anything. Now you think I am in your power, and you will do nothing; but, sir, if you don't comply with my demands, I will instantly blow your brains out."[161]

"You dam'd cowardly dog, take that door, or I will kick you out of it," Van Dorn demanded as he looked away and back to papers on his desk. Dr. Peters drew his pistol, aiming to shoot the General in the forehead, but he turned and the shot went behind his left ear causing him to convulse and shudder. His left arm was on his lap, blood was flowing from the back of his head against the glass in the window next to his writing desk. A piece of writing paper was on the desk, a pen still wet with ink, and the inkstand near the General's right hand. Dr. Peters was convinced that he had killed him instantly, picked up what was written for evidence, and immediately left the house to go to Shelbyville to turn himself into General Leonidas Polk. Since Polk was a relative of Dr. Peters' second wife, he did not think that he would be arrested.[162] Not only was Polk related to his second wife, but Dr. Peters' brother Thomas was serving as quartermaster under Polk.

Fountain Kerr Odel reached the front steps of the Major Cheairs' home when he heard three muffled gunshots "like someone stomping on the floor with his foot…" Almost immediately, Dr. Peters appeared at the door with a smoking pistol in each hand. He stood and looked at Odel for a moment and then struck a dog trot toward the Presbyterian Church located north of the house where his horse was hitched.[163] Sol Gregory, who had just been given a dispatch to be carried to General N. B. Forrest who was 16 miles south of the Tennessee River, was in the yard of the Martin Cheairs' residence when he heard the shot fired.[164]

---

161 *Op. Cit.*, Voluntary statement.
162 *Ibid.*
163 *Op. Cit.*, William Ewing Fowler.
164 Frank A. Smith Interview of Sol Gregory on November 4, 1907 *History of Maury County, Tennessee,* compiled by Maury County Historical Society. 1969. p. 29.

Neely McMeen, the overseer of the farm, came running around the corner when Odel asked, "Neely, is there going to be a battle?"

"Battle?" he questioned. "Yes, Dr. Peters just killed General Van Dorn."[165]

Joseph Henry Fussell's company was in the saddle when General Frank Armstrong told him to go at once to Van Dorn's headquarters. His command was just north and had to go in a gallop through the streets of Spring Hill to get to the Cheairs' home. Fussell dismounted and went in alone to find Mrs. Cheairs and a black cook in the hallway. They told Fussell that Van Dorn had been shot. When he entered the room, Van Dorn was sitting at the desk with his arms on it, his head bent forward, but still breathing. A pistol ball had entered the back of his head near the base of his brain. It did not come through his face but was lodged just above or below the eye because the eye was protruding. Fussell lifted up the General's head and blood ran out of the wound on to his collar and back. Mrs. Cheairs told Fussell that Dr. Peters had shot Van Dorn and left the house by the rear with the pistol still in his hand as if he were going to his own home located across the back. Fussell sent out details to look for Dr. Peters but were unsuccessful mainly because they did not have the desire to catch him.[166]

Several officers entered the room and assisted Milton, the body servant, move the General to his bed in the northwest corner of the room.[167] The General died that afternoon, and Brig. General William H. Jackson assumed command of the cavalry under provisions of General Orders No. 1.

Dr. Peters followed an old road that went around a lake and by his home. Jessie met him at the front door, and Dr. Peters told her, "I

---

165 *Op. Cit., William Ewing Fowler, p. 191.*

166 Frank A. Smith Interview of Joseph Henry Fussell, aide-de-camp to General Frank Armstrong, one time candidate for Tennessee Governor, October 18, 1906 *History of Maury County, Tennessee,* compiled by Maury County Historical Society. 1969. p. 119.

167 Emily Van Dorn Miller, *A Soldier's Honor with Reminiscences of Major-General Earl Van Dorn,* (The Abbey Press: 1902), p. 351-352.

have shot General Van Dorn, and I am going to join the Yankees." He then changed directions and promptly rode out Davis Ford road.

A servant who witnessed the scene was said to have reported, "Miss Jessie just stood there with her hands on her hips and said, 'Now ain't that the devil, a sweetheart killed and a husband runs away--all in the same day!'"[168]

Dr. Peters rode out and turned up a road where he met an older man astride a horse. He demanded that the man go with him and direct the way to the Duck River bridge. The man refused until Dr. Peters drew a gun and frightened the man into leading him. Riding a very old horse at a rapid pace, it fell dead before they reached the destination although he directed Dr. Peters the rest of the way.

An hour after the murder, Jackson's adjutant, Captain Moorman, sent for Isaac Nelson Rainey. He was asked if he knew Clara Peters, the daughter of Dr. George Peters, who was a student at the Columbia Athenaeum. He responded that he did, after all, he had attended the school as a child of eleven when a few boys were allowed to attend. Isaac was given a letter about the circumstances of what Dr. Peters had done. He was directed to ride as quickly as possible and deliver the message to her at once. He rode the eleven miles in one and one-half hours, saw Clara, delivered the note, and did not tarry. Although Isaac had frequently seen General Van Dorn and other dashing young officers on their fine horses riding with Jessie, he described his death as a "most cowardly and dastardly assassination."[169]

In a letter written by a student, it stated that Jessie Peters came to school to get Clara and General Van Dorn was with her. There were some family members who believed that he actually was after Clara. She was asked if she knew the General, but she responded that she had only met him once.

---

168 *Op. Cit., William Ewing Fowler, p. 191.*
169 Written by I. N. Rainey in 1922 when he was in his eighties.

General Earl Van Dorn. The back has Monumental Photograph Company, Baltimore, Maryland. Courtesy Rippavilla Plantation donated to them by Scott Smith.

White Hall where General Van Dorn had his first headquarters in Spring Hill. His room was on second floor, last room on right obscured by tree. Privately owned by Jean and Joe Ed Gaddes for events.

White Hall staircase where Jessie Peters brushed by Mrs. White to go upstairs to introduce herself to General Van Dorn. Courtesy of Jean and Joe Ed Gaddes.

House inherited by Jessie where she and Dr. Peters stayed while in Spring Hill and General Van Dorn was caught visiting Jessie. The house burned in 1957. Photo in the collection of Maury County, TN historian, the late Jill Garrett.

SEASONS IN THE SOUTH

Martin Cheairs, who allowed General Van Dorn to move his headquarters from Dr. White's to his home that was the location of the confrontation of Peters and Van Dorn. He was Nathaniel Cheairs brother, who was married to Susan McKissack, Jessie's sister. Photo courtesy of Rippavilla Plantation, Spring Hill, TN

Martin Cheairs home that was General Van Dorn's headquarters where he was shot by Dr. Peters. Known today as Ferguson Hall on campus of Tennessee children's Home.

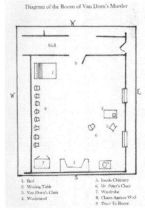

Diagram of the room in which General Van Dorn was killed.

General Van Dorn's Funeral and Aftermath

A most impressive and solemn funeral was held the next day. The command was mounted and drawn up on each side of the street by 8:15 the next morning to pay respects and to watch the hearse and the honor guard start on the trip to Columbia. Laid inside of the hearse drawn by six white horses with an array of black and white plumes was the metallic casket that carried the body of the General. At the head of the coffin peacefully rested was his Mexican sombrero bearing a gold Texas star with his gold-hilted sword, a present from the State of Mississippi. Stretched below the sword were standing his military boots. Following the hearse was the General's horse, bridled and saddled. As the hearse passed down the line, the officers and men saluted their dead leader with their saber. Although it was extremely quiet, many cried in silence. It was tremendously evident in Van Dorn's escorts who were men of the old Army. They had followed the dashing "Major" into the Confederate Army.[170] His body was taken to the Maury County courthouse in Columbia where his remains were viewed by admiring comrades. According to the records of Lamb & Barr

---

170 Victor M. Rose, *Ross' Texas Brigade*, (Louisville: Courier-Journal 1881), p. 101.

Undertakers, Major Paul paid $175 for the coffin made of wood in Columbia.[171]

Over six feet tall with dark hair and eyes, Captain Thomas Walker Davis was from Davidson County and served in the 1st Tennessee Cavalry. He recorded in his diary on Thursday, May 7 that he was startled at an early hour by the intelligence that General Van Dorn was dead. At first he thought it was rumors, but "on every breeze the unwelcome rumor came." It was told at first that Dr. Peters cut the General's throat, but a ball lodged over the left eye causing death a few hours later. "The Citizens and soldiery sympathize with Peters." Captain Walker recorded on Friday, "The 1st Tennessee escorted the body of our late lamented General to Columbia. A salute of three vollies was fired over his sepulcher. General Van Dorn was a brilliant man, but he was addicted to pleasure and licentiousness, which destroyed his usefulness."[172]

Mary Polk Branch, a cousin of James K. Polk, met the General just weeks before at a ball given for the officers at the home of Leonidas Polk known as Ashwood Hall. It was before the Federals maneuvered into the Columbia area, and now she was attending the General's funeral.

Of course the funeral was a military one, but as the procession passed south to Rose Hill Cemetery from Columbia, she described how solemn, the band played, the blare of trumpets, his powerful black horse that was riderless, and on each side the inverted boots of the late gallant officer, and the hearse drawn by six white horses.[173] Services were held in St. Peters' Episcopal Church before his body was temporarily deposited in the family vault of the General Lucius Polk's first wife and mother of all his children. She was a Donelson

---

171 "List of Interments During Civil War," taken from Lamb & Barr Undertakers, Book begins November 14, 1862.
172 Thomas Walker Davis Diary, Capt. Co 5 1st Tennessee Cavalry, Davidson County native. Entry on 7th Thursday.
173 Mary Polk Branch, *Memoirs of a Southern Woman*, Property of University of North Carolina, Chapel Hill, N. C. (Chicago: Joseph G. Branch Publishing Co., December 1912), p. 26.

cousin, Rachel Jackson being her aunt as she was also an aunt to General Van Dorn's mother.[174]

General Van Dorn could not be buried in his hometown of Port Gibson because it was occupied by the Federals. His remains were transported by train with members of his staff to Mount Vernon, Alabama and buried in the Godbold family plot on his in-laws estate. A staff officer told of the General's little daughter was the chief mourner visible at his bier. His wife was too despondent by grief to leave her room but was seen looking from the window. The burial was about forty yards from the house, and little twelve year old Olivia clung to the officer's hand.[175]

Ten days after Van Dorn was killed, his personal items including the sword given to him by the state of Mississippi were sent to his wife who was living with her mother just north of Mobile. Two years later following the capture of Mobile, the plantation was raided by Union troops of the 7th Illinois. One of the plantation servants tipped off the captain of the raiding patrol that a box containing swords and guns was buried on the grounds and pointed out the spot. The Union soldiers dug up the spot and found two of Van Dorn's swords and a three barreled revolving gun. One of the swords was taken by the captain and neither was heard of again. The gold mounted sword presented by the state of Mississippi was taken home by Sergeant Burt Moses. Nineteen years after the war, Moses was living in Iowa and offered to sell the sword to the state of Mississippi for $250. The state of Mississippi felt that they should not have to pay for an item that was from the loot of a raid. In 1950 Harold C. Books of Marshall, Michigan, wrote T. W. Crigler, Jr. of Macon, Mississippi, commandeer-in-chief of the Sons of Confederate Veterans, that he would buy the sword from the Moses descendants and return it to Mississippi as a gift. The sword was placed on exhibit in the restored old Capitol[176]

---

174 St. Peter's Episcopal Church, Columbia, TN, Church records, May 8, 1863.
175 *Op. Cit., Miller,* p. 253.
176 "The Sword of Gen. Van Dorn," Know Your State, Ray Thompson, *The Daily Herald*, Mississippi, November 29, 1961.

In a letter from Harold C. Brooks, who owned an appliance company, he stated that he had purchased the sword in 1941 from Mrs. Roy Myers. She gave a statement indicating, "My grandfather captured it during the siege of Vicksburg," but then went on to say that "negroes were hired to divulge places of hidden treasure." The sword was in a velvet lined case and was unlikely to have been captured in a battle field but rather looted. The letter also indicated that the sword had been made by R. Fitzpatrick.

Dr. Peters crossed the bridge, cut back, and traveled across the country to reach the Cumberland River. He had fled to Shelbyville anticipating being pardoned by General Leonidas Polk since he was related to Dr. Peters' second wife. His brother Thomas was a major serving as quartermaster under Polk, but when he arrived he found that the authorities were not only going to arrest but incarcerate him.[177] He was disguised by Major J. J. Murphy, a personal friend from Memphis, who gave Dr. Peters a pass through the Confederate lines. He was going to Kentucky for coffee and sugar for the officers. Passing the lines, he made his way to the Federal camp at Gallatin.[178] Therefore, he returned to Nashville within Federal lines by way of McMinnville that was about 40 miles northeast of Shelbyville and Gallatin that was northeast of Nashville. Crossing the river, his horse drowned, and if it had not been for the Yankee soldiers who swam out to get him, he may have also met the same fate. They started to hang Dr. Peters for being a spy, but after he told them that he had killed General Van Dorn, they decided to wait for a few days until the truth could be determined.[179]

Lum Biggers, who joined the Union after his brother was killed by Van Dorn's men, was serving as a Union soldier on picket duty when Dr. Peters entered the Federal lines. They knew each other, and Dr. Peters was grateful to find him at this intense time. Lum escorted Dr. Peters to General Gordon Granger's headquarters in

---

177 *Op. Cit.*, Peters' Voluntary Statement.
178 *Op. Cit.*, U. S. National Archives & Records Administration.
179 *Op. Cit.*, Fowler.,

Nashville.[180] Giving a statement about the entire event, Dr. Peters renewed the oath because when he had left Spring Hill, he did not get his certificate of having taken the oath of allegiance in Memphis.

After the death of General Van Dorn, there were numerous opinions about his death and the conditions that led to his premature loss of life. Many felt that he was inefficient as a leader and let alcohol and women be more important in his life. Even some his own men indicated that when they were sent to look for Dr. George Peters for the murder that they did not look too hard to find him. In a letter sent by P. B. Starke, commanding officer of the 28th Mississippi Cavalry to President Jefferson Davis from Columbia, Tennessee, May 11, 1863, it stated:

To President Davis
My Dear Sir
Since my telegraph to you, I have taken some pains to ascertain what were the particulars in regard to the shooting of Gen'l Van Dorn by Dr. Peters, and have but little to add. After conversing with one of the late Gen'l's staff officers I find that Dr. Peters was moved to kill the Gen'l in consequence of his familiarity with Mrs. Peters, visiting her and remaining at her house until late hours of the night—and that in the absence of the Doct. The impropriety of this conduct was freely discussed and condemned in and out of the army. That he was a gallant soldier and patriot is conceded by all. The only question discussed is as to the manner in which he was killed. The Doct. went into his room and found him alone. The firing of a pistol caused his staff to go in to the room. They met the Doct. coming out, who mounted his horse and rode rapidly away.
I did not see the body but it is stated by his friends that he was shot in the back of the head and it supposed that the Gen'l was sitting at his table when the Doct. shot him from behind. That the Gen'l had great weaknesses in such matters must be admitted. The corps under Gen'l Jackson is doing well, but we all feel great anxiety as to the gen'l who is to

---

180 *Op. Cit.*, Lynch.

be permanently in command. My own regiment is in fine condition and will when the occasion occurs equal their charge into Franklin.

Gen'l Van Dorn said that was the most gallant performance he ever saw. I am still presiding over the gen'l court martial. My kind regards to Mrs. Davis,

One report from a source of implicit confidence stated that Van Dorn's character was infamous. Some years ago he deserted a beautiful and devoted wife, and took up with a filthy, drunken, degraded harlot. Without giving details three days after Van Dorn's death, this is the only reference that he may have been involved with another woman besides his wife.

General St. John Richardson Liddell was a prominent Louisiana planter although he was born to a wealthy plantation family in Mississippi. He had been a schoolmate of Jefferson Davis. In his recollections of the War, he wrote about Van Dorn:

> We had been at Mrs. Erwin's but a short time when Hardee told the company of the death of General Van Dorn with the attendant circumstances. I had already heard the facts, but had not thought it proper to mention them. The character of the general was discussed, and the common opinion was clearly expressive of condemnation. Little or no regret was felt for a man whose willful violation of social rights led him to such an inglorious end. He had started with the full confidence and favor of the people and president. At Corinth, Van Dorn after repeated failures with his corps (Price and others under him) had finally to acknowledge his incapacity for so large a command (for which he deserves credit)...In utter recklessness at his fallen state, Van Dorn gave way to passions that soon ruined him.[181]

Will C. Nelson, a classmate of Thomas Peters at the University of Mississippi, wrote to his father from near Fredericksburg, Virginia on May 12, 1863:

---

181 Nathaniel Cheairs Hughes, Jr., *Liddell's Record*, (Louisiana: Morningside House, Inc., 1985), p. 121.

Providence will raise up other leaders march us on to victory, but it will be long before General (*Stonewall*) Jackson's place is filled.

How different his death from that of Van Dorn, and how different the emotions excited by the two. One receives the tears of a nation, for he was a good, as well as a great man, the other a Drunkard and a libertine, is thought to have met his just doom. I see by the papers that he was killed by Dr. Peters of Hardeman County. Was it Tom Peters' Father?[182]

Emily Van Dorn Miller, sister of the General, wrote a book in 1902 that included many letters from his staff and friends praising his performance as a soldier. She asserted that the murder was a conspiracy by Dr. George Peters and his wife Jessie Helen McKissack Peters because of their loyalty to the Union and attempt to keep their property.[183] One on Van Dorn's staff was his nephew Clement Sulivane and another who admitted that he started the rumors to protect the reputation of the General.

M. H. Kimmel, Major and Van Dorn's adjutant related to his son in 1913 that Van Dorn had been killed in a cabin on the Peters' plantation. To protect his name and reputation, they moved the General to his headquarters late at night in an ambulance when no one would notice. When search parties were out looking for Dr Peters, Kimmel decided to circulate the story that Peters was an enemy agent under orders to kill Van Dorn. This anecdote was told fifty years after it occurred to the son and another fifty years before it was related to Arthur Carter.[184] Thus far no other notation has been recorded of a similar incident although details of finding the General at his desk are consistent with witnesses who found him in his headquarters. Dr. Peters was recognized by several local

---

182 Jennifer W. Ford, *The Hour of Our Nation's Agony*, (Knoxville: The University of Tennessee Press, 2007), p. 124.

183 Emily Van Dorn Miller, *A Soldier's Honor with Reminiscences of Major-General Earl Van Dorn*, (New York: The Abbey Press, 1902), p. 249-255.

184 Arthur B. Carter, *The Tarnished Cavalier*, (Knoxville: The University of Tennessee Press, 1999), p. 186-189.

citizens, and the reporting of the shooting was also by the presence in the house of Mrs. Cheairs, her small child, and a servant.

While Dr. Peters was in Nashville shortly after the shooting, Kimmel reported that friends of Dr. Peters took the occasion to write Governor Isham Harris asking for a pardon because the sanctity of the home was being protected. Newspapers reported similar information, and witnesses said that Jessie and the General had been seen several times on carriage rides. As a practical politician, Harris gave a pardon before any trial or hearing was held.[185] Dr. Peters had also been in the state legislature during the time that Harris was governor. When the legislature had been moved to Memphis the year before because Union troops took Nashville, Harris more or less gave up governorship of the state and became Aide-de-camp to Albert Sidney Johnston and Joseph E. Johnston.

The *Memphis Daily Appeal* said that they received a dispatch on May 9 from John S. Whitfield, Provost Marshall concerning the death of General Van Dorn had been confirmed and to arrest Dr. Peters for the murder. They gave a description of Dr. Peters as about six feet tall, dark complexion, dark iron-gray hair, black eyes, and whiskers on his chin that were a little gray.[186]

John Bell Brownlow wrote a letter on October 25, 1901 concerning his experience with Dr. Peters just days after he killed General Van Dorn. He was rooming at Ben Weller's large boarding house on Clay Street. Ben was also a tinner and cooper and had men boarding in the house who did the same kind of work. Ben asked John if he would share his room with a man who had tried to get a room at the St. Cloud Hotel and others, but they were too crowded. He could recommend him, and as a favor to him, would he share his bed for one night? The room was on the floor above the basement where the dining room and kitchen were located. It was called the first floor, but the distance from the window sill to the ground was too great for one to hurt another by shooting through the window unless he stood on a ladder.

---

185 *Ibid.*, p. 189.
186 *The Memphis Daily Appeal*, Saturday, May 9, 1863, p. 1.

Dr. Peters did not get to the room until about 8:00 pm because he was attempting to get permission from the military authority to go to St. Louis but had been refused. For several hours and until midnight, this man told in detail his troubles and every facet of the shooting. His conversation was rational, but he labored under great mental excitement, and expressed a fear that some friend of General Van Dorn's in Nashville would assassinate him if he stayed in that city. John tried to calm him down by saying that no one would try anything in a city full of Union soldiers. They both retired for bed about twelve but left a very small light from a gas burner. Within half an hour, John was awakened by a gunshot, and all the gas lights in the room were fully turned. Dr. Peters jumped out of bed thinking that he had seen an assassin at the window and shot at him. He was against the wall in his night clothes, barefooted, and with the pistol leveled and pointing at the window. He was shaking so badly that it was like someone with palsy. John shouted at him, "Don't point that dammed pistol this way! Why are you there and why did you fire?"

Since only one shot was fired, it had to be Dr. Peters. He talked in such a wild and crazy way that John tried to assure him that no one shot, and he was hallucinating. Because the pistol was not going to be given up, John regarded Dr. Peters as temporarily insane and sat up with him the rest of the night. The day after the experience, John got his father William G. Brownlow to get Dr. Peters the permit enabling him to go to St. Louis. Under the regulations then existing, the permission was necessary.[187]

In a letter to his wife dated July 13, 1863, John told her that "an attempt was made at our boarding house last night to assonate Dr. Peters by firing into his window with a pistol, missing his head but a few inches. It is supposed to be some rebel in the employ of Van Dorn's staff officers." William G. Brownlow was known as "Parson" and was a strong Unionist from East Tennessee and later served as governor after the war. John commanded the Union's

---

187 *Op.Cit*, Emily Van Dorn, pp.349-350.

9th Regiment of Tennessee Cavalry, served as special agent for the United States Treasury Department, and worked for the post office in later years. With his son in 1904, he started Knoxville's first real estate firm.[188]

After Dr. Peters was released in Nashville while it was in possession of the federals, he was able to come around to Memphis by boat and arrived home about June. Shortly afterwards, General Buford, who was located in Helena, sent for him to come down and give him some information about the crossing of some Confederate troops that he thought had passed by his plantation. They had crossed 20 miles away after the rebels had taken everything on the place. Although he was told to consider himself under arrest, he was given a pass the third day.[189] In the diary of a niece of Martin and Nathaniel Cheairs, brother-in-law of Jessie Peters, she writes in July about how she and her grandmother and some others had to leave Springfield, Missouri because of fighting during the War and make their way to Arkansas. They encountered Dr. Peters coming from his home.[190] Near the end of the year, he went down about fifty miles below Helena to the McNeal place where his niece lived to buy some cotton and was arrested the first night.[191]

Lieutenant Dan H. Alley, Co. G. 3rd Texas Cavalry was in command of General W. H. Jackson's scouts. In the fall of 1863 with five men, he was on an investigative expedition in Bolivar County, Mississippi. One evening after striking camp, the men scattered out among the houses of the immediate neighborhood with two or three in one place. Walter Boster and another man went to a house

---

188 "John Bell Brownlow," Biography/History, University of Tennessee, Knoxville, Special Collections Library.

189 U. S. National Archives & Records Administration, RG 123, Cong. #3690, George B. Peters, Southern Claims Commission, Application, Abstract for Special Agent, Box 484, April 22, 1876.

190 *A Confederate Girlhoods: A Woman's History of Early Springfield, Missouri*, Edited by Craig A. Meyre (Moon City Press: Springfield, Missouri, 2010), p. 31.

191 *Op. Cit.*

about a mile away. When Boster reported back, he stated that he thought Dr. Peters was at the house where he was stopping but not sure. Alley instructed him to return and keep watch throughout the night and arrest him if he were sure beyond a doubt that it was Peters. After supper, the ladies of the family and Dr. Peters, were engaged in a game of whist. The lady of the house was a niece of Peters, and one accidently called him by name. Shortly after this, he laid off his pistols on a table allowing Boster to arrest him. Dr. Peters made no resistance although appeared very much incensed at such a procedure. He sent out a servant messenger to Alley wanting him to come to the house and explain. Alley sent Boster instructions to guard Dr. Peters until morning and then he would come.

When Alley arrived early the next morning, Dr. Peters demanded to know Alley's authority for causing his arrest. Alley explained that he was a Confederate officer, and Dr. Peters was being arrested for the killing of Major General Earl Van Dorn since there was a standing order for his arrest. Dr. Peters wanted to know what outlook Alley would make of him. Alley stated that he reported to Brigadier General W. H. Jackson and Peters was destined to that officer's headquarters.

Dr. Peters maintained that he knew that the Texas Brigade had intended vengeance against him, and Alley was a Texan and intended to do away with him. Alley assured Dr. Peters that he would be protected as long as he remained cooperative. Dr. Peters slept very little or none and wrote the greater part of the night. On the way to the headquarters, he talked freely about the affair and was more critical of his wife than Van Dorn. He told of how this was not the first time his wife had been unfaithful with another man, he had separated from her, but he stayed with her because of the children.

Dr. Peters recounted how he caught Van Dorn at his house two nights before the killing. Van Dorn ran out and under the house with Dr. Peters in pursuit and dragged him out by his hair. Van Dorn was intoxicated and begged for his life. Dr. Peters spared him on condition that he would visit his house no more, sign writings to that effect, and admit in writing that he had been too intimate with his wife. On the morning of the killing, Dr. Peters went to Van Dorn's headquarters, but Van Dorn refused to comply; therefore, he was killed.

Alley took Dr. Peters to General Jackson's headquarters about fifteen miles from Canton, Mississippi. They tried to take Dr. Peters away from him, but Alley refused to the point of opposing any attempt and threatening to kill the prisoner himself rather than give in to their forces.[192]

On November 13, General Jackson sent a message to J. A. Seddon, Secretary of War in Richmond:

> Our cavalry has arrested and sent in the murderer of Major-General Van Dorn, a citizen. What course can be taken? There are no courts for us in Tennessee.[193]

General Jackson had Dr. Peters sent to Meridian, Mississippi, where the court was in session for the trial of all military causes.[194] He was confined for three weeks and released by General Johnston. He decided that since Dr. Peters did not belong to the Army that he would have to be tried in the civil courts. Dr. Peters claimed that he went to Atlanta and gave bond to Governor Isham G. Harris. He knew Harris personally since they had been school mates probably in Winchester, Tennessee at Carrick Academy for male education. He indicated that he would appear in Maury County at the first time of court after the close of war. From there he went to Memphis.[195]

According to a newspaper account, Dr. Peters was brought before Honorable William Kilpatrick at Okolona, Mississippi on a writ of habeas corpus on November 25. Okolona is about 124 miles north of Meridian. He was tried, acquitted, and returned

---

[192] Victor M. Rose, "Capture of Dr. Peters," *Ross Texas Brigade,(1881), p. 99.*

[193] *Official Records of the Army, XXXI, Pt. 3, pg. 689.*

[194] Voluntary Statement of Dr. George B. Peters, "Annals of the Army of the Cumberland," 1864. pp. 618-620.

[195] *Op. Cit,* U. S. National Archives & Records Administration.

home to Arkansas. In his testimony before the Southern Claims Commission, he was released by a writ of habeas corpus obtained by some friends and old acquaintances previous to the war. Another account indicates that the case was dismissed for lack of evidence.[196] General Forrest was in Meridian on November 4 when he received orders from General Joseph E. Johnston that he had assigned him and his small force to western Tennessee. He reached Okolona on the 15th. It is quite possible that he testified for Dr. Peters or at least signed an affidavit. His attitude towards Van Dorn was not on the best terms. Miss Laura Galloway in whose home Forrest stayed while in Columbia, Tennessee, heard Forrest tell her father how he hated Van Dorn, and would like to "cut his heart out and STOMP it."[197] Because no files exist, speculation is the only source.

It was the understood attitude that if a man caught his wife with another man, the husband was justified in taking the man's life. At this point, no record has been found of the proceedings or any listing in the *Official Records of the Army*; however, Judge Kilpatrick was born in Maury County and probably was an acquaintance of Dr. Peters. His father was a Methodist minister in the area and Dr. Peters' grandfather was also and was known to have campgrounds for meetings and interpretations of the Bible. They both left the area about the same time although Dr. Peters was a few years older than Kilpatrick. During the War, General Leonidas Polk had his headquarters in the Kilpatrick home located in Corinth, Mississippi.[198] After he killed Van Dorn, Dr. Peters made an attempt to go to Shelbyville where Polk was at that time. Polk was related to Dr. Peters' second wife and felt that he would receive some assistance, but there was already a warrant out for his arrest.[199] The majority of accounts indicate that there was a lack of

---

196 *Ibid.*
197 Frank A. Smith Interview of Mrs. Minnie Towler and Miss Laura Galloway, June 27, 1904 *History of Maury County, Tennessee*, compiled by Maury County Historical Society. 1969. p. 119.
198 *Cross City Connections*, Vol. 16, No. 4, June 2008, p. 18-19.
199 *Op. Cit.*, Voluntary Statement of Dr. George B. Peters.

evidence to convict Dr. Peters. It must have been considered a civil case and not a military, but knowing Judge Kilpatrick no doubt assisted Dr. Peters through the court system.

Chickasaw County has Houston and Okolona as their county seats. During the War when the Federals were in the Okolona area, residents took all the files from the courthouse but were stopped on the outskirts of town. All the files were burned and there is no reference in the *Official Records of the Army*. Dr. Peters' name is not mentioned in any capacity.

Col. Freemantle was quoted in *Tennessee's War* as to the death of General Van Dorn:

> His loss does not seem to be much regretted as it appears he was always ready to neglect his military duties for as assignation. In the South, it is not considered necessary to put yourself on an equality with a man in such a case as Van Dorn's by calling him out. His life belongs to the aggrieved husband and 'shooting down' is the universally esteemed and correct thing, even if it takes place after a lapse of time, as in the affair between General Van Dorn and Dr. Peters.

By the summer of 1862, Helena, Arkansas, in Phillips County had been captured and occupied by Federal General Samuel R. Curtis and remained in the hands of the Union Army throughout the balance of the war and some years after the end of the war. A futile attempt was made by the Confederate Army on July 4, 1863. The residents in the area had an enormously difficult time. After the war, carpetbaggers took over to make the local residents even more uncomfortable. St. John's Episcopal Church was once more open after four years, and the members returned doing the best that they could do not knowing what each day would bring.[200]

Dr. Peters had his own problems trying to maintain his personal

---

200 Excerpts from Diaries and letters of Reverend Otis Hackett from the files of St. John's Episcopal Church, Helena, Arkansas, Furnished by G. H. Hackett, Phillips County Historical Quarterly, Vol. 1, No. 1, Summer 1962, p. 36.

property, and the health of his oldest son Thomas was a major concern. There was an indication in the files that the resignation of Lieut. T. M. Peters was offered on a surgeon's certificate of disability on the same date that he gave a resignation. He was dropped from the rolls about thirty days without sending in a proper document. He could be "gotten rid of by general orders" because there was no board decision, and he was absent. The notes claimed that Thomas Peters was in Arkansas unable to move. The person reporting stressed that they had no doubt that he had forwarded the certificate, but the papers had not reached them. It would possibly be better for him, and when the board command was convened, they "respectively requested that evidence of his gallantry in the force be presented."[201]

Capt. W. L. Scott, Corp of Light Battery wrote a letter from the field on October 17 to Colonel George William Brent, Assistant Adjutant General. He stated that although Second Lieutenant Thomas Peters was assigned to his duty on January 3, 1863, from that time until the present, he had not performed more than two weeks duty in the company due to ill health. On June 8, he received sixty days leave of absence based upon a surgeon's certificate. Since that time, he had not been officially heard from and had been reported absent without leave as required by law. He made application for the appointment of an Examining Board as required in such cases by the act of Congress "to relieve the Army of disqualified, disabled, and incompetent officers."[202]

A monthly report dated on April 1, 1863, that gave the officers and men absent with leave stated that a thirty day furlough had been granted by General Bragg on March 20. On May 1, 1863, Thomas' muster roll card indicated that he was in Shelbyville, Tennessee. Just seven days later his father would kill General Van Dorn for his relationship with Thomas' stepmother.

---

201 Thomas M. Peters, 2nd Lieutenant, Confederate file under Capt. Scott's Company, Tennessee Light Artillery, 1863.
202 *Ibid*

In October 1863, from Council Bend, Arkansas, Thomas wrote a letter to General S. Cooper:

Sir

I have the honor to offer resignation as 2nd Lieutenant Scott's Battery Cheatham's Division Polk's Corps, Army of Tennessee.

Thomas M. Peters

On October 23 a statement in the files states that a board is necessary because the officer is absent without leave and "could be gotten rid of by General." M. T. Polk sent a letter relating that he knew unofficially the condition of Lieutenant Peters. His health was serious, and he was in Arkansas unable to move. He further stated that he had no doubt that he had sent forward certificates but had not reached their destination. He felt that if he were relieved from active duty—honorably, it would be better for him, and when the Board was convened, he respectively requested that they consider the gallantry in service. He needed to be released to his family in order that they could take care of him. Polk did not believe that he would ever recover and would probably die at home.[203]

Dr. Peters obtained a permit from Union General Hurlbut to bring his wounded son to Memphis to tend to him.[204] Three doctors from Memphis wrote a letter on October 29 relating to Thomas' condition. Dr. William Vannah Taylor, age 73, educated at the University of Pennsylvania, came from North Carolina and finally settled in Memphis in 1848. He had been a Navy Assistant Surgeon in the War of 1812. Just four months before, he wrote to Major General Hulburt requesting to be released from taking the oath in hostility against his children because he had sons in the Confederate Army. He had a fully disabled wife, a lady friend suffering from pulmonary consumption and confined to bed, and did not have means to relocate elsewhere. Dr. A. K. Taylor age 43

---

203 *Ibid.*
204 *Op. Cit.*, U. S. National Archives & Records Administration.

also came from North Carolina, and Dr. John Pitman age 55 was born in Virginia. The following is their diagnosis:

> We the undersigned practicing physicians of the city of Memphis certify on honor that Lieut. Thomas M. Peters formerly of Polk's Battery Army of Tenn. a young man 21 years of age called on us this day to consult us relative to the state of his health. He has been laboring under intermittent fever for several months past at this time occurring daily. His health is likewise suffering from disease of the genital system requiring medical treatment and probably a surgical operation. In view of the actual condition of his health and the intense mental anxiety under which he labors, we are of the opinion that he should be relieved of duty by resignation or furloughed until his health can be restored.[205]

In the first stage of syphilis, a small, painless ulcer appears, usually on the genitals. Several weeks later, the second stage is marked by temporary fever and a rash that clears up spontaneously. The patient may then feel well for years until the third stage develops. As the fatal stage, the infections consume the brain, blood vessels, and many other vital organs. In the *Medical and Surgical History of the War of the Rebellion* published in the 1880s, there can be confusing statements because three venereal diseases—syphilis, gonorrhea, and lymphogranuloma venereum—appear to be mixed together in the record and perhaps occurred simultaneously in patients. Lymphogranuloma tends to produce plumsized swellings in the lymph glands of the groin. These swellings are termed "bubos," and when they burst and drain, pus was described as suppurating bubos.[206] Treatments were varied, but none would last because of the absence of antibiotics.

---

[205] Dr. John P. Patton, III a retired radiologist who lives in Meridian, Mississippi, and has a strong interest in the War Between the States, gave his professional opinion after reading the letter that it was syphilis and the patient was very young when he got the disease.

[206] Thomas P. Lowry, M.D., *The Story the Soldiers Wouldn't Tell*, (Pennsylvania: Stackpole Books, 1994), p. 102-104.

Although the papers are dated as to the time that they were written, it is next to impossible to determine when they reached the proper person. It has always been the opinion that the circumstances that surrounded Dr. Peters in May were the cause of Thomas' deteriorating mental condition. If Thomas went to Council Bend to be with his family, it is unknown who took care of him other than servants. His father was still to some extent on the run, his brother in the Confederate Navy and a prisoner of war about that time, his sister in school at the Athenaeum in Columbia, and his stepmother in Spring Hill, Tennessee, awaiting the birth of her fourth child. Other relatives would have been in Bolivar and not Arkansas. He was more than likely administered to by servants who were located at the plantation. His Army records indicated that he was home unable to move. As a physician, Dr. Peters no doubt knew that his son was in serious condition when he made his way back home with him.

The family of Martin Cheairs whose home was the scene of Van Dorn's death and his brother Nathaniel Cheairs, who was married to Jessie Peters' sister, had been residents of Spring Hill when Dr. Peters' family was also located in the area. Their sister Louisa had married at 17 to John Polk Campbell, a very tall for that time period of six feet and two inches in height with light brown hair that curled and eyes that were keen and jovial. They moved to what is today Springfield, Missouri, where they were among the earliest settlers. John Polk and Louise donated fifty acres for the construction of a town in 1833 with two acres designated as the public square.[207]

During the War, Louise and her youngest son, a granddaughter, and some others including a number of servants made their way to Helena, Arkansas, in an attempt to reach another sister where she felt that they would be safer from advancing forces. As they were traveling north, the granddaughter described an old man coming from a pretty well-kept house. He grasped her grandmother's hand

---

[207] Martin J. Hubble, *Personal Reminiscences and Fragments of the Early History of Springfield Green County Missouri*, (Springfield: Inland Printing Co. 1914), pp. 31-45.

crying, "Lucy Cheairs, where did you come from, and what are you doing here?" After telling him her story, Dr. Peters invited them into his house and served them breakfast of broiled chicken, hominy, waffles, and coffee with rich cream. After their ordeal, it was such a pleasure for these refugees to sit at the lovely set table and be served such a generous meal. After a long rest, Dr. Peters sent a boy with them to reach their destination about eight miles away.[208]

Actions in Arkansas had become very inadequate since the majority of the units had been reduced from the state for service east of the Mississippi River. When General Thomas C. Hindman arrived in Little Rock, Arkansas in May 1862, he found that his command was "bare of soldiers, penniless, defenseless, and dreadfully exposed" to the Federal Army that was dangerously close from the northwest. The Confederate Congress had authorized destroying cotton, tobacco, military supplies, and any other property in danger of falling into the hands of the Union Army.[209]

General Hindman had sent an order to Dr. Peters to burn all the cotton that he could get. When he refused, an order was issued to hang Dr. Peters on the first tree or bring him to Little Rock. There were men on the lookout enabling Dr. Peters to escape; however, he was almost caught while fishing in Lake Mallicote.[210]

Apparently, the stress was beginning to physically take its toll on Dr. Peters. The incident occurred in July 1863 after the death of Van Dorn in May. He had made his way back to his plantation while anticipating his destiny. He probably was not aware that his son James Arthur, who had served in the Confederate Navy until June 17, 1863, had been captured with the others at Wassaw Sound by two monitors in trying to run the blockade. He was a prisoner

---

[208] Sheppard, Louisa Cheairs McKenny, *A Confederate Girlhood*, unpublished manuscript, 1892. Sarah Rush Owen Papers, History Museum of Springfield; Green County, p. 31.

[209] Neal, Diane, *The Lion of the South: General Thomas C. Hindman*. (Macon, Georgia: Mercer University Press 1997), pp. 118-119.

[210] *Op. Cit.*, U. S. National Archives & Records Administration.

at Fort Warren, a 28 acre Georges Island prison at the entrance to Boston Harbor. It served as a prisoner-of-war camp and jail for political prisoners. He escaped from the facility once but was recaptured to spend another year there before being released.[211] Dr. Peters learned that relatives of Arthur's mother had sent him $200 when they asked for the replacement of the money.[212]

Maury County Tennessee on Christmas Day in 1863 passed with a cloudy wind from the South that turned into rain that night with the wind changing directions. Within three days, the rain would be mixed with snow early in the morning. Nimrod Porter, who had been sheriff in Maury County, wrote in his diary how robberies were committed everywhere. Soldiers belonging to both armies and those who did not belong to any army were trafficking and trading unlawfully. They were hiring blacks to steal mules and horses for them that caused those left in their homes with nothing.[213]

The new year started the morning with a clear and extremely cold day with some snow. The heavy rains of the previous day had flooded the ground that was now a sheet of ice and snow. Soldiers continued to take mules, horses, and swept the county of stock.[214] Jessie would soon be twenty-six and was expecting her fourth child. Her stepdaughter Clara must have still been in the area since Robert Smith, whose family ran the Athenaeum school where Clara attended, mentions in his diary that on Christmas Day 1862, he was near Franklin and got a furlough from Maj. General Pat Cleburne for 24 hours to go home to Columbia. He mentions seeing Clara on the road as he was going to Columbia. She was also at school in the Athenaeum in May when a soldier brought her a note about her father shooting General Van Dorn. The convent in St. Lewis where

---

211 James Arthur Peters, Midshipman, Official Records of Confederate States Navy.

212 *Op. Cit.*, National Archives.

213 Nimrod Porter, Maury County, Tennessee Sheriff, Diary entry January 1864, p. 120-126.

214 *Ibid.*

she completed her education stated at the time of her death that she came there while her home in Bolivar was "then endangered by the Civil War." The *St. Louis Times* during 1868 alluded to her coming to the city to devote herself to the church that "every calamity that war may beget has befallen her family, kindred, fortune, and home." The residence in which she lived since childhood was in the path of the destroying army, and most of the property was destroyed. She and an only brother, no doubt George, Jr., had encountered many tragedies as they wondered among strangers.[215]

The weather had been very cold and at times there had been snow on the ground but had finally cleared and warmer almost like summer. Jessie did not have a husband to comfort her during this difficult occasion. She had sisters nearby, Dr. Aaron White was still assisting in the area, a few servants, and her other two children William almost five and Lucy two years. Jessie turned 26 on January 3, 1864, and the baby arrived twenty-three days later, 264 days or thirty-seven weeks and five days, or as some counted eight and half months after Dr. Peters killed General Earl Van Dorn. She named the baby girl Medora Wharton Peters. A very rare first name, Medora means ruler, but she would usually just be called Dora that was no doubt a constant reminder of the name Van Dorn.

---

215 "The Saddest Story of the Cruelest of Wars, "*The Nashville Republican Banner*, Vol. 54, No. 147, Nashville, Tennessee, June 25, 1868, p. 4.

Dr. Peters' Grown Children

By November 1864, James Arthur Peters was paroled, and within a month, exchanged at Cox's Wharf, Virginia. Sometime later, he was promoted passed midshipman of the Provisional Navy of the Confederate States. He was on temporary duty at Drewry's Bluff on the James River, Virginia by February 1865 where he served aboard the *CSS Richmond*.[216]

This ship was part of a class of six ironclad rams built at the Norfolk Navy Yard. As the Confederates prepared to evacuate the Norfolk area, she was towed up the James River to Richmond, Virginia and completed in July 1862. She served in the James River Squadron protecting the Confederacy's capital city from waterborne assault. She was intentionally destroyed by burning on April 3, 1865, as the Confederate Government prepared to abandon Richmond. James attached as 1st lieutenant, Company 1, 2nd Regiment, Admiral Raphael Semmes' Naval Brigade by April. He surrendered and was paroled at Greensboro, North Carolina, on April 26, 1865, seventeen days after the War had ended.[217] James would eventually live on some of his father's land in Council Bend, Arkansas, that was to be known as Peters Landing.

Whatever treatment that the doctors did for Thomas, he

---

216 *Op. Cit.*, James Arthur Peters.
217 "CSS Richmond," Department of the Navy, Naval Historical Center, Washington, DC.

recovered enough to go to Coffeeville, Mississippi, to study law under Major General Edward Walthall.[218] Walthall studied law and started practicing in Coffeeville after being admitted to the bar in 1852. He was district attorney for the 10th judicial district before he joined the Confederate Army and served in the same areas as Thomas. After the War ended, he resumed his practice in the law office with Colonel Lamarr about 80 miles south of Memphis until he moved to Grenada six years later.[219]

G. L. Morphis was a representative in the Tennessee State Legislature at the same time that Dr. Peters was serving as a senator. He wrote a letter about seeing Dr. Peters only once after the Legislature was adjourned. On his way to Oxford, Mississippi in the fall or winter of 1865, he encountered a man who had been riding in front of him. He was on a poor mule with an old army saddle and a large roll tied behind. He wore a slouch white hat, a very much worn suit of clothes, and realized it was Dr. Peters. They rode together several hours and during that time, Dr. Peters related how he had heard that Van Dorn's staff officers had declared their intentions of killing him if they ever saw him. He was attempting to get to his plantation on the Mississippi River by way of the Alabama mountains and hills of northeast Mississippi to avoid publicity as much as possible.[220]

There had always been rumors that General Van Dorn's staff had taken a pledge to kill Dr. Peters. The following card was published in the Mobile, Alabama, newspaper on May 15, 1863, just eight days after Van Dorn's death:

---

218 Thomas Peters' Obituary, The *Bolivar Bulletin*, Bolivar, Hardeman County, Tennessee, April 14, 1866, p.1.
219 Edward Cary Walthall 1831-1898, Biography of United States Congress, 1774-Present, Office of Art and Archives, Office of Historian, Washington, DC.
220 "Letter From G. L. Morphis, *Nashville Banner*, April 1, 1913, first published in Cleveland, Oklahoma.

The Late Gen. Van Dorn—A Card From His Staff

Editors Advertiser and Register:

We the undersigned, members of the late Gen. Van Dorn's staff, having seen with pain and regret the various rumors afloat in the public press, in relation to the circumstances attending that officer's death, deem it our duty to make a plainstatement of the facts in the case.

Gen. Van Dorn was shot in his own room of Spring Hill, Tenn., by Dr. Peters, a citizen of the neighborhood. He was shot in the back of the head, while engaged in writing at his table, and entirely unconscious of any meditated hostility on the part of Dr. Peters, who had been left in the room with him apparently in friendly conversation, scarce fifteen minutes previously, by Major Kimmel. Neither Gen. Van Dorn nor ourselves were suspicious in the slightest degree of enmity in the mind of Dr. Peters, or we would certainly not have left them alone together, nor would Gen. Van Dorn have been shot, as we found him five minutes later sitting in his chair, with his back towards his enemy.

There had been friendly visits between them up to the very date of the unfortunate occurrence.

Gen. Van Dorn had never seen the daughter of his murderer but once; while his acquaintance with Mrs. Peters was such as to convince us, his staff officers, who had every opportunity of knowing that there was no improper intimacy between them and for our own part, we are led to believe that there were other and darker motives from the fact that Dr. Peters had taken the oath of allegiance to the United States Government, while in Nashville, about two weeks previously—as we are informed by refugees from that city—that he had remained in Columbia, a short time before, "that he had lost his land and negroes in Arkansas, but he thought he would shortly do something which would get them back," and finally, that having beforehand torn down fences and prepared relays of horses, he made his escape across the country direct to the enemy's lines.

Such is the simple history of the affair, and we trust that in bare justice to the memory of a gallant soldier, the papers that have given publicity to the falserumors above alluded to—rumors alike injurious to the living and to the dead—will give place in their columns to this vindication of his name.

> H. M. Kimmel, Maj. A. A. G.,
> W. C. Schaumburg, A. A. G.,
> Clement Sulivane, Aid-de-Camp,
> R. Shoemaker, Aid-de-Camp.[221]

Thomas wrote a letter to Major Wright C. Schaumburg on February 23, 1866:

> Sir:
> The prevalence of a rumor throughout the country of this import that you and your associates of Van Dorn's Staff not satisfied with having published the most infamous Card ever presented to the American people, have pledged yourselves to take the life of my father Dr. George B. Peters, induces me to make an inquiry of you as to its truth.
> My father is ready at any time to be tried by the Courts of the Country if any prosecution is made.
>
> Address me, care of Maj. Henry Hampton, Memphis
> I am Sir Very Respectfully
> Thos. M. Peters[222]

Living in New York, Schaumburg responded on March 14:

Your letter dated Coffeeville, Feb. 23d, 1866, is received

---

221 "The Late Gen. Van Dorn—A Card From His Staff," Mobile, Alabama, newspaper. May 15, 1863.
222 Thomas M. Peters to Major Wright C. Schaumburg, February 23, 1866, in Emily Van Dorn Miller Papers, Mississippi Dept. of Archives and History, Jackson, Mississippi.

and after considering the matter I have decided to overlook the bad taste of your denouncing a card which has my signature in the same communication in which you ask of me information—and in justice to myself to answer your question lest by silence I may be misunderstood, I have never known of any pledge made by any member of Gen. Van Dorn's Staff to take the life of Dr. Peters, nor have I ever heard of any such intention on their part. The members of the Staff, Sir, were gentlemen and brave men, a fact which had you duly appreciated would have been in itself an answer to your question.

As regards the Card to which among others my signature was added I have only to say that it contained statements which I at the time believed to be true, and since the publication I have had no cause to change my opinion. I did not at the time suppose "the card" would please Dr. Peters or any of his friends.

Respectfully
Yr. obdt. svt.[223]

A resident of Cambridge, Maryland, Clement Sulivane, Aide-de-Camp and nephew of General Van Dorn, wrote a letter on March 12 to Thomas after hearing of the correspondence with Schaumburg that states:

Thos. M. Peters, Esq.,
Sir:
My friend Maj. Wright C. Schaumburg of New York City has this day put me in possession of a letter of date of Feb. 23d addressed by you to him, and from circumstances which I will at one state, without the slightest reference to any action of his, I deem it my duty to write to you.

You will pardon my interfering in this matter when I inform you that I was a nephew of the late Gen. Van Dorn, that I was an officer upon his Staff at the time of his murder, that it was I who drew up the statement of

---

223 Wright C. Schaumburg to Thomas M. Peters, March 14, 1866, Emily Van Dorn Miller Papers, Mississippi Dept. of Archives and History, Jackson, Mississippi.

facts concerning that murder which you are pleased to term "an infamous card" and which I signed along with other gentlemen whose integrity you know, if you know anything, is beyond suspicion. I therefore suggest that if you have aught to complain of in connection with that affair it will be with more propriety that you address yourself to me.

In relation to your intimation that the Courts of the country are open and that Dr. Peters is ready and willing to abide his trial, I have to inform you that the propriety of a prosecution has been discussed by the family of Gen. Van Dorn and only given up or postponed as you will by a knowledge by the fact, as well known to you as to us, that in the present political state of Tennessee, when every office from high to low is filled by the bitter enemies of the Confederate Army, any attempt to bring Dr. Peters to trial for the murder of a Confederate Officer of high rank would be worse than useless, a mere force when we remember that every Confederate soldier's life was forfeited by the very law under which it is proposed to try a man for shooting one. It is to this state of affairs that Dr. Peters owes his escape thus far from the penalty of his crime. It may prove unwise in you to persist in agitating matters which, having yielded to force of circumstances we have consented to lay at rest. Having no feeling of <u>vengeance</u> in the matter we are content to leave my Uncle's assassin to the pangs of his own conscience.

Having said this much it is almost unnecessary to say further that I have never even heard before of the absurd rumor you mention that we (the officers of Van Dorn's Staff) have pledged ourselves to slay your father. <u>We</u> are not assassins, and I think I can speak for the rest at the same time that I speak for myself when I state that, having escaped us at the moment of his crime, such a design against him as you enquire into has never been entertained for a moment.

I have no desire to hurt your feelings unnecessarily, you being a perfect stranger to me of whose existence even I was not aware before the receipt of this letter, but I feel called on to speak plainly and courteously in regard to a most serious matte you have unnecessarily revived old memories and have yourself to thank if you, perforce, hear the truth. It is not unnatural that a young man, as I judge you to be, should feel keenly any allusions to so delicate and distressing a tragedy in which your father was a principal active and the ladies of your family were concerned (by public rumor) but that you may understand these things once for all, I will state the cause that led to the publication of the card alluded to above. You will find what I state here also recapitulated in a letter to Col. Marsh Polk, written about the 25th of May, 1863.

It was bruited about in a number of newspapers that Dr. Peters had shot Gen. Van Dorn for criminal connection with his wife and daughter, and to put a stop to the foul slander one who was familiar with all the circumstances and knew the falsehood of the report determined to publish over my signature a brief statement of the real facts and of my views in relation to them. This we did and I think we succeeded, at least I heard nothing more of the thing afterwards. The facts as we stated them in relation to the murder and its surrounds were <u>true</u> and can be substantiated before a court of justice, and I take the liberty of suggesting that it is unmanly and ungenerours, without you are prepared to contravene it by proof, to call that statement "infamous" in letters to men 2000 miles off whom you well know you would not dare thus address face to face. The <u>precedent</u> circumstances I should think it madness in you to endeavor to establish in contradiction to our car the <u>immediate</u> circumstances attending the murder (Dr. Peters last visit, the shooting, &c.) are stated by us on our honor a soldiers and gentlemen and it would be foolish in you, who knew nothing about it to gainsay them and the reports concerning his visit to Nashville, &c. we spoke of <u>as reports</u> which prevailed at the time we believed them, but whether they were actually true or not we would not pretend to assert.

Thus, Sir, I have given you succinctly what had been to me a painful preview of some of the circumstances attending the unfortunate transaction which occasioned your letter to Maj. Schaumburg and mine to you. If well advised you will not seek further to kindle and inflame old recollections, but in all events I must insist that it is I who am mainly concerned in this affair and not Maj. Schaumburg. I have therefore to request that if you will persist in pursuing this correspondence, you will address yourself to me and not to him.

> I am very respectfully
> Your obedient servant,[224]

Clement Sulivane was described by by his uncle as "my favorite nephew." After the war, Sulivane returned to Maryland and resumed his law practice and became a journalist and state senator. Three years later, he married Delia Bayly Hayward and had three children. None of their children married or had children of their own.[225]

The first of April, Thomas traveled through Memphis, and then a short distance south to his father's plantation in Council Bend, Arkansas, close to the Mississippi River. His friends thought that he looked unusually well while he visited them and gave no indication about the extreme mental anguish that he was experiencing.[226] However, Dr. Peters may have discussed with him during the visit that he intended to divorce Jessie.

When Thomas returned to Memphis on Sunday night of April 8, he stayed upstairs in the store of Pitser Miller. As a young man, Pitser had been a very well respected and a wealthy merchant in Bolivar. He established P. Miller & Co. in Memphis on Second Street with Thomas R. Smith, who had married Sarah Catharine Miller. She had attended the Columbia Institute in Columbia, Tennessee, and her father had served on the board of the Columbia Athenaeum during and after the War.[227] Another Pitser Miller was a Bolivar attorney just a few years younger than Thomas.

---

224 Clement Sulivane to Thomas M. Peters, March 12, 1866, in Emily Van Dorn Miller Papers, Mississippi Dept. of Archives and History, Jackson, Mississippi.

225 Frank Collins, "Clement Sulivane Biography," East New Market Page, Collins Factor, 2005.

226 *Op. Cit.*, Thomas Peters' Obituary.

227 Female Institute records, *The Guardian,* 1848, Catalogue 1866.

The gentlemen who were with him indicated that "he was in a pleasant humor, and his mood was as agreeable as was the habit of this young gentleman." He left them, went upstairs where he had been the night before, placed his shawl carefully on the floor, and arranged a pillow. He gently polished his boots, combed his hair, carefully dressed in a complete uniform of a commissioned officer of the Confederate States Army, buttoned the coat to his chin, lay down on the shawl, placed a pistol with the muzzle behind his ear, and fired (a year to the day that the War had ended). The men ran up the steps to find Thomas slightly quivering with little blood on the pillow and the shawl undisturbed. He had written two letters to his parents and another one to someone else.[228]

The family escorted the remains from Memphis to Bolivar, and Bishop Quintard noted in his journal on Wednesday, April 11, 1866:

> Left Memphis for Bolivar to officiate at the funeral of Mr. Thomas Peters. At night in St. James Church, Bolivar, after evening prayer by the Rector, I preached. Returned to Memphis on Thursday.[229]

At 12 noon the body was taken to St. James Episcopal Church where Dr. Peters had been a member, and Jessie had made an elaborate impression upon the members when she first moved there. After the imposing ceremony at the church, the coffin was followed to the Polk Cemetery where Thomas was buried near his mother.[230] Three days later Dr. George B. Peters would file for divorce in Helena, Phillips County Arkansas.

An article concerning Claire returning to St. Louis two years later indicated that she lived to "soothe a father's sorrows and lighten anguish that almost dethroned his reason." She had been divinely

---

228 *Op. Cit.*, Distressing.
229 Journal of the Annual Convention, Diocese of Tennessee by Episcopal Church Diocese of Tennessee, Published by the Diocese, Easter 1866, Wednesday, April 11.
230 *Op. Cit.*, Distressing.

inspired, and with her soft, sweet voice never lost its tenderness. She saw her father's grief become despondent and the church his resource.[231]

On April 17, Dr. Peters filed a Bill of Divorce from Jessie H. Peters in Phillips County Arkansas Circuit Court. It declared that she was a non resident of the State of Arkansas and announcement of the suit be published for a certain number of times in the *Western Clarion*, a newspaper published in the city of Helena. In Chancery Court, the records indicate that Jessie failed to appear. Until the 1st day of May, 1863, the parties cohabited together as husband and wife when Jessie abandoned Dr. Peters' "bed and board without just cause or provocation and continued to absent herself there from ever since."

Thomas Hawkins and John B. Cobb swore in open court that "the facts set up in said bill and above stated are true…"[232] A Thomas Hawkins had lived in the area just north of the Peters' plantation. John B. Cobb was certainly Dr. Peters' brother Thomas' former brother-in-law who was born in Franklin County, North Carolina in 1810 and eventually lived in Jackson, Tennessee. He had previously lived in Fayette County where he was engaged in cotton planting with investments in Arkansas. He had been living in Obion County where his first wife Miss Peters had died. He had one daughter and eventually remarried[233] Another source listed his wife as Lucy, and Dr. Peters had a younger sister by that name. The divorce was granted, and their rights were restored as they existed before their marriage. Dr. Peters had to pay all the court costs in the execution of the suit. [234]

Clara, daughter by Dr. Peters' second wife, had finished her

---

231 *Op. Cit.*, The Sadist Story.
232 Phillips County, Arkansas Circuit Court, George M. Peters, Complt. vs. Bill of Divorce Jesse H. Peters, p. 90.
233 *The Forked Deer Blade,* John B. Cobb Obituary, Jackson, Tennessee, October 25, 1884.
234 *Op. Cit.*, Phillips.

education at the Academy of the Visitation in St. Louis, Missouri. The Academy of the Visitation was started in 1799 in Georgetown that is now part of Washington, D.C. Their school was a free school for the poor, based on the best European girls' schools, and there were individual classes for free blacks and slaves. Most were not Catholic, and the school expanded throughout the United States and St. Louis. After several establishments, the sisters in 1858 set up a campus at 19th Street and Cass Avenue on 13 acres given to them by Anne Biddle, a wealthy benefactor who had helped them when they arrived in St. Louis. During the War, Visitation Academy had a record 160 boarding students who included a daughter of Union General W. T. Sherman and two nieces of Confederate President Jefferson Davis.[235]

William Tecumseh Sherman's wife was a devote Catholic and graduated from the Visitation Academy in Georgetown, D. C. with high honors of graduating number six out of forty-three. She raised her children in the same way although her husband did not always agree concerning religion. They had moved about before the War but had moved to St. Louis in 1861 in order that he could be head of a street car company but only for a few months before his military involvement.[236]

A niece of Martin and Nathaniel Cheairs attended the convent in St. Louis after the War. She was behind in her school work and anticipated being able to advance under the direction of this school. In her memories of that time, she mentions paying $110 in Confederate money for sprigged merino that was a soft wool and cotton fabric. She and her grandmother went to New Orleans to buy clothes that she would need for school. She bought russet button boots, a soft grayish brown coat, and a grey hat with blue tips. A dressmaker would make a black silk alpaca for a school uniform, a grey silk dress for the street, and a lovely soft white nun's veiling for her best wear among other things that she would need.

---

235 Barbara Watkins, "Visitation Academy: 175 Years and Still Going Strong," St. Louis Review Online, May 23, 2008, p. 2.
236 *Ibid.*

The Academy girls were given supply lists and in an 1880 list, the following was given as necessary:

> For the summer uniform, two black alpaca dresses, four light-colored shirt waists, and three white shirt waists will be required; and for the winter, two dresses of black merino, or other woolen material, and six wash aprons—not white—all made in a plain style. Additional requirements included 24 Pocket Handkerchiefs, 6 Pairs of Summer Stockings, 6 Pairs of Winter Stockings, 6 Changes of Underclothing, 4 Night Dresses, 2 or 3 Pairs of Shoes, 1 ¼ yards Black Net, for Veils, 1 ½ yards Wash Blonde, for Veil, etc[237]

At the beginning of the War, the majority of the population in rural areas and the South had almost no knowledge of the Catholic sisterhood. During the War, many nursing nuns cared for the sick and wounded in the Union and Confederate soldiers in the military hospitals. A woman's life in a convent released her from the demands of marriage; however, a training nun had to be totally obedient to God, to her superior, and to the rules of order. A very strict day included an observance of the rule of silence at all times except during a brief recreation period set aside each day. In addition to the work for the order, she spent the rest of the day and evening reciting prayers, meditating, saying the rosary, attending mass, listening to spiritual readings during meals, and examining her conscience. She was not allowed to develop a friendship or special fondness for any particular sister or enjoy close family relationships. If a young nun survived the difficult entry period, she took her vows of poverty, chastity, and obedience and became an official member of the order. Most nuns of this time were teachers and nurses while others cared for orphans and the indigent elderly.[238]

Clara finished her education and questioned the virtue of the

---

237 *A Confederate Girlhoods: A Woman's History of Early Springfield, Missouri*, Edited by Craig A. Meyre (Moon City Press: Springfield, Missouri, 2010), p. 59.

238 Judith E. Harper, *Women During the Civil War: An Encyclopedia*, (Taylor & Francis Group: New York 2007), p. 74.

sisters. She was a fervent Protestant, upright and intelligent. She knew that there would be great sacrifices, but she decided that she would devote her life to God by becoming a nun. The St. Louis *Republican* reported on December 17, 1869 that Clara had assumed the black veil the day before in the elegant chapel of the Convent of the Visitation with Miss Jane Sheppard about twenty years of age assuming the white veil during the ceremony. Crowded with ladies and gentlemen, it had been a year since Clara entered the Order and assumed the white veil. She took the name Mary Paula, and her personal charm and graciousness drew everyone to her.[239]

The habit worn by the ladies was very simple: black with long white sleeves; their veil was plain and black. They wore a black band over the forehead and a guimpe (a short-sleeved blouse worn under a pinafore or jumper) of white linen descending nearly to the waist without any fold. A silver cross on the breast and a black rosary in the girdle completed the attire. She outlived her father and all her brothers, but no mention is made of her again.[240]

She took her vows in 1868, and it is quite possible that she was the "someone else" to whom Thomas had written a letter before his suicide. An article about her life with a brother whose sorrows made him insane, and he put a period to his own existence indicated that they wandered among strangers when every species of property was destroyed. The house in which she had lived since childhood was in the path of the destroying army.[241]

George B. Peters, Jr., was only eight years old when his father married Jessie and was too young to fight in the War as his two older brothers. The first indication that he was in school in Bolivar was a teacher who returned after the War to open a school about three weeks later.

---

239 Sisters of the Visitation, B.V.M., From our Monastery of St. Louis, Missouri, November 30, 1917.
240 Michael D. Cassidy, "Visitation Convent and Academy," Roman Catholic Institutions, p.9
241 *Op. Cit.*, The Sadist Story.

Opened a summer session of Bolivar Male Academy in railway station on May 31, 1865. The Academy building had been defaced by the Federal Army to such an extent that it was untenable, and we had no cars running for more than three months. So much changed had conditions become that of the 66 pupils in school in May 1861 only four: James Neely, Jr., George B. Peters, Jr., James Fentress, and Charles A. Miller returned to greet in 17 of 66 entering the army, 14 as members of Company E and 3 as number of other commands, 4 of the 14 were killed in field and all others served till the close of war. Eleven of 17 are dead, and 6 are living. Station was pleasant place and boys anxious for instruction that I was teaching 7 hours or days. They wanted Latin, Greek, and mathematics.[242]

John Milton Hubbard was headmaster of the Bolivar Male Academy when he left with 101 largely young men to join Company E 7th TN Regiment Forrest's Cavalry Corp. Many more enrolled as they had service in five states; however, many of their original group dropped out and abandoned the cause.[243]

George, Jr., must have completed his education enough to enter Washington and Lee University because he graduated at the age of 20 in 1870. General Robert E. Lee had been president of the university since the end of the War, but he was to die in October of the same year. He apparently knew George who was valedictorian of his class[244] and received five gold medals upon graduation.[245] George came home and entered Cumberland University law school in Lebanon and graduated a year later.[246]

The year following the War had been on the whole strenuous for Dr. Peters. He had lost his oldest living son to suicide, divorced his third

---

242 John Milton Hubbard, *Notes of a Private*, (E. H. Clarke & Brother: 1909), p. 180-181.
243 *Ibid.*, p. 1.
244 "Shelby County," *History of Tennessee*, (Nashville: The Goodspeed Publishing Co. 1887), p. 1022.
245 *Memphis Daily Appeal,* August 15, 1869.
246 *Op. Cit.*

wife, his daughter had joined a convent never to have a family to come together with other descendants, and a confrontation with another land owner. In November both men were in the vicinity of Marion, Arkansas, that was just across the river from Memphis. James O. Lusby was listed as being from Council Bend, although just previous to the War, he was living in Fayette County, Tennessee, just east of Memphis. It was stated in the Nashville Banner that a misunderstanding had existed between the two for several months. An adjustment had been attempted and there had been a court proceeding, but there had been no satisfaction in the matter. Dr. Peters also lived in the area and had vast amounts of land in his possession.

In the courts and upon overtaking Dr. Peters in Marion, Mr. Lusby began attacking him with a cane that he had in his hand at the time. After being assaulted, Dr. Peters did not have a weapon except a pocket knife that he used to thrust at Lusby cutting his throat and severing his windpipe. The wound began to bleed profusely at which point Lusby threw down the cane and pulled a derringer from his coat and fired at Dr. Peters. Throwing up his arm in protection, the bullet went through the right sleeve of his coat. Realizing that he had not wounded his victim at that point, Lusby pulled out a six-shooter and was about to shoot when Dr. Peters ran to a nearby store building. It probably saved his life since Lusby was becoming very weak from the slash to his neck and fell from exhaustion. Several standing nearby picked him up and transferred him to get medical assistance. A Dr. Maddox, who was close to the area, was summoned to give assistance, but he and others declared that the injury was fatal since the wind pipe had been completely severed. Dr. Peters gave himself up to the authorities when he learned of the seriousness of the situation but volunteered to sew the gash up that led to saving of Mr. Lusby's life.[247] He lived almost another year and died in Fayetteville, Arkansas. His wife Elizabeth, whom he married when she was fourteen, died two weeks later.[248]

---

247 "Fatal Affray in Arkansas," *Nashville Republican Banner*, Vol. 53, No. 50, November 16, 1866.
248 "Deaths," *Arkansas Gazette*, Little Rock, Oct. 15, 1867.

Clara Polk Peters known as Sister Mary Paula Peters. Guerin in St. Louis took the picture. His son George would marry Medora Peters Lenow's daughter Kate. Photo courtesy of Archives of Visitation Nuns located at Visitation Academy in St. Louis, Missouri with assistance from Lisa Chassaig.

Visitation Convent and Monastery, Cabanne, St. Louis. Moved here in 1892. Today known as Visitation Park with only the gym building retained for recreation. Clara Peters remained here until her death on Nov. 30, 1917. Postcard circa 1900.

Thomas McNeal Peters, Dr. Peters' son by his second wife. He was a student at University of Mississippi when he left to join the Confederacy. University of Mississippi 1861 Senior Class Book in possession of Archives and Special Collections of UM.

Jessie McKissack Peters graduated from the Athenaeum in Columbia, Tennessee in the Class of 1853. Her stepdaughter Clara Peters was a student in May 1863 when she received a note that her father had killed General Van Dorn. Photo courtesy Athenaeum Rectory, Columbia, TN.

General Van Dorn's Families and Children

About a week after leaving Mobile Alabama, a Federal Unit had just received an official notice of the fall of Richmond and surrender of Lee. They were all rejoicing knowing that the war would soon end. For two or three days, the Army camped near the residence of Mrs. Godbold, the mother of Caroline Van Dorn. They described the house as a two story frame house that had been painted white. They knew of the prominent General in the Confederate service and the cause of his death. Dr. Johnson who was with the unit described Caroline as living in the quiet lonely region, retired from the world, and no companions except her mother.[249]

Eleven years after the war on January 19, 1876, Caroline Godbold Van Dorn would follow her husband in death and be buried next to him. The *Washington Gazette* stated that "In a cemetery near her native place she sleeps by the side of her loved and noble husband whose loss she mourned as only those who knew him best could mourn him." At the head of his grave was a board that had been inscribed:

> Blow winds your softest above the bed
> Where sleeps the dearest among the myriad dead[250]

---

249 Charles B. Johnson, *Muskets and Medicine or Army Life in the Sixties*, (Philadelphia: F. A. Davis Company, 1917), p. 227-228.
250 Mrs. Caroline Van Dorn, *Holly Springs South*, Deaths, March 16, 1876.

Earl Van Dorn's son by the same name wrote a letter to his Aunt Emily informing her of his mother's death. He mentioned the letter that he received from his aunt thanking her for her efforts in getting him employment. He did not feel that he was capable of any kind of responsible business due to his inferior education would cause him to be at a loss as what to do. He was going to leave Alabama since there was nothing more dear to him since he lost his mother. He looked on his aunt as a second mother.[251] Earl was a subcontractor on the railroad west of the Mississippi River in Monroe, Louisiana. Because of an exposure incident related to his business, he got pneumonia and died on April 30, 1884. His funeral was held in the Episcopal Church where a large number of local citizens gathered to honor him. His casket was decorated with the flowers of early spring. He was buried in Monroe Cemetery and the residents of the city strewed flowers over his grave for the sake of his father.[252]

About five years after the death of her father, Olivia at the age of sixteen, the same age that her mother had married her father, would marry Frank Aubrey Lumsden in Mobile, Alabama. Frank's ancestors had started the *Picayune Newspaper* in New Orleans, and his father was a newspaper reporter, but Frank preferred being a steam boat clerk. They had two girls and two boys; unfortunately, Olivia died after the birth of her fourth child on February 4, 1878. She was buried beside her parents at her request just two years after the death of her mother. The house in which they lived was taken for a surety debt following the death of Caroline's father. Frank purchased the home but resold it to Dr. W. T. Webb. Frank went on to marry two more times and had another child who lived just over a year. He went from being a steam boat clerk to a captain before his death in 1911.[253]

In June 1878, General Joseph Wheeler of Lawrence County, Alabama had a statement printed in the *Mobile Register* asking if anyone knew the whereabouts of General Earl Van Dorn's children.

---

251 *Op. Cit.*, Miller, p. 20
252 *Ibid.*, p. 19.
253 *Op. Cit.*, Miller.

Not until 1914 was a settlement of an account made of Earl Van Dorn who had died intestate but had left interests in Mobile, Alabama that was a claim against the United States Government in the amount of $1000. It was due for "military services rendered by him while serving in the United States prior to 1861 as an officer in the United States Army." He was considered a resident of Mobile, Alabama at the time of his death. Carrie L. Clemmons filed with the court that she was the granddaughter and asking that she be appointed to the administration of the estate that now totaled $1031.80. The others included Charles A. Bolhman, Tunstall Lumsden, Carrie L. Clemmons, and Lillie Earl Ballinger. Each received $194.25.[254]

Earl Van Dorn's sister Emily had his remains removed in November 1899 and reburied in Wintergreen Cemetery in Port Gibson, Mississippi, next to their father. She did not disturb her sister-in-law's remains in the Godbold family plot. It could have been that there was little appreciation for Earl's wife, but it would have been an easier situation if both had been moved.[255]

In recent years, all the graves had to be relocated because of the location of a new manufacturing company in the area.[256]

After Van Dorn's death, Martha Goodbread married a man by the name of Bird. Court records indicate after the death of her father in 1872 that Martha is dead and has minor children. Her sister Elizabeth married Jacob Degan, and it is he who has custody before 1872 according to a court document relating to the estate of her father. It is not known at the present when she died, where she is buried, or any other information about her husband. Records indicate that the children were raised by their grandparents, but Martha's brother-in-law Jacob Degan had custody. The children always said that they were orphans. Douglas, who herded cattle and farmed, married Lou Asie Heathcock on May 29, 1880, and had

---

254 Mobile, Alabama Probate Court, Consolidated Judicial Division Index Minutes, Volume 48, 1914-1916, pp. 7-8.
255 *Op. Cit.*, Carter, p. 199.
256 "Artifacts found at the possible site of industrial plant", Andy Netzel, Press Register, Mobile, Alabama, November 21, 2008, Front page.

twelve children. Lammie Bell married James T. Carr on August 4, 1877, and had three children. The oldest Percy died in September 1879 when his horse was thrown by a cow that he had roped. The horse fell on him causing injuries that contributed to his death two days later.[257]

Caroline Godbold Van Dorn's grave. All the remains were removed to a new location. Photo courtesy of Barbara N. Cope, Texas.

Cemetery where General Earl Van Dorn was buried near Mr. Vernon, Alabama. His sister Emily had his remains moved to Port Gibson, Mississippi in 1899. The flag draped tombstone marks where he was buried. Caroline's grave is on the left of the tree. The cemetery was located across from Caroline Van Dorn's home place. Courtesy Barbara N. Cope, Texas.

---

257 Barbara Cope, Dallas, Texas, Great Granddaughter of Martha Goodbread in a 2010 interview.

SEASONS IN THE SOUTH

Percy and Douglas Van Dorn, sons of Martha Goodbread and General Earl Van Dorn. The children went by Van Dorn name. Photo courtesy of Barbara N. Cope, descendant of Douglas.

Lammie Bell Van Dorn Carr, daughter of General Earl Van Dorn and Martha Goodbread. Photo courtesy of Barbara N. Cope, Texas.

Death certificate of Lammie Bell Carr indicating that her father was General Van Dorn. Courtesy Barbara N. Cope, Texas.

Recovery After the War

Reverend Otis Hackett wrote in his diary in January 1866 that old Helena was not what he remembered in happier times. The old buoyancy of spirit was gone. The grand "difficulty that perplexes the wisest and staggers the most hopeful is the labor question. The planters would gladly hire the Negroes at remunerative wages, but it is felt and found that they cannot be depended upon. As their own masters, they are restless, shiftless, and idle. They are slow to learn that there can be any connection between liberty and labor…Our people…are very poor having lost everything amid the disorders of the late unhappy war." Reverend Hackett went to see a man who formerly attended the church and was quite active. The man was embarrassed about not attending church. He did not have clothes and would not attend unless he could be decently dressed.[258]

In the June 1866 issue of *The Guardian* at the Athenaeum, Dr. Peters is listed under Friends and Patrons living in Council Bend, Arkansas. Also listed were numerous officers and soldiers who fought in the War: General Nathan B. Forrest, who stayed in a house near the entrance of the Athenaeum and was given a ball by the Smiths; Dr. T. E. Moore, who was in medical practice with Dr. Peters in

---

258 Excerpts from Diaries and letters of Reverend Otis Hackett from the files of St. John's Episcopal Church, Helena, Arkansas, Furnished by G. H. Hackett, Phillips County Historical Quarterly, Vol. 1, No. 1, Summer 1962, p. 39.

Bolivar; and William B. Bate, who was wounded at the Battle of Shiloh and became governor after the War, and Bishop Quintard, who conducted the funeral of Clara's brother Thomas. Thomas Peters died two months before the issue, and their father had already filed for divorce. Pitser Miller, whose business in Memphis was the location of Thomas' suicide, was a member of the Board of Trustees.

Dr. Peters' brother Thomas lost a vast amount of fortune by the time the War had ended, but this did not deter him from eventually recovering from other interests. He began exploring in mountainous areas in Alabama for ores and coal. He traveled throughout unknown forests locating mineral lands and opening the way for cultivation. He went to Savannah, Georgia, and entered the cotton trade, but he returned to Jefferson County, Alabama, in 1869 to live in Elyton while engaging in mineral land speculation.[259]

Thomas was an early settler of the region and along with others is credited with establishing Birmingham. He took charge of the exhibit made by the Alabama railroads from their lands and those adjoining the Louisville exposition of 1883. Because of overwork and a severe attack of cold, he died at the infirmary. He was brought back to Birmingham to be buried in Oak Hill Cemetery. He outlived his only child Amelia and her husband Robert Henley, who was the first mayor of Birmingham.[260] It was said that Thomas was very well known and pleasantly remembered as he was a distinguished tall commanding figure with iron gray hair and beard.[261]

The Nashville *Republican Banner* of July 9, 1868 carried this report:

> Dr. Peters, widely known as the man who shot and killed General Van Dorn of the Confederate Army during the War for alleged intimacy with Mrs. Peters, was in this city

---

259 Owen, Thomas McAdory, LL.D, *History of Alabama & Dictionary of Alabama, 1921*, 1349.

260 Thomas S. Tate, "Major Thomas Peters: A Man of the Early Days," *The Birmingham Ledger*, July 11, 1903.

261 Matilda E. Cressman, "Major Thomas Peters," *Early Days in Birmingham*, (Alabama: Birmingham Publishing Co. 1937), p. 71.

one day this week in company with the quondam Mrs. P. The long estranged couple are now said to be on the best of terms, and it is reported that the broken marriage vows are soon to be renewed.

Dr. Peters and Jessie remarried in Bowling Green, Kentucky, on July 9, 1868. It was about three weeks after Clara assumed the black veil. Family history had always indicated that he sent for her to come to Arkansas, but he told her "do not bring that child." The 1870 census records do not have Medora listed in the family at the post office of Columbia, Tennessee. William age 11, Lucy age 8, are listed along with Kate Chalmers age 12 who was born in Mississippi. Dr. Peters' sister Susannah Hill Peters married Col. William Arthur. Their daughter Rebecca Jones Arthur married the Confederate General James Ronald Chalmers.[262] After the war, he returned to his law practice in Mississippi and was a United States Representative. They had two daughters named Kate and Irene.[263] Another source listed four children and included Dora Chalmers who married Henry Lenow of Memphis, and Clara Chalmers, who entered a convent in St. Louis.[264] Although the last names should have been Peters, the other information is correct. Since they were living in Austin, in the county of Tunica, Mississippi, it was located just over the river about twenty miles from the Peters' plantation and could have been living with the family.

Jessie and her sister Lucy Hudson, who was a little over three years older, attended the Columbia Institute from which Lucy graduated in 1851. The Athenaeum opened in 1852, and Jessie graduated from there a year later almost four months after Lucy married William Pope Parham.[265] After four boys, they had their second daughter on April 30, 1867, whom they named Winnefred

---

262 Boddie, John Thomas, *Boddie and Allied Families*, 1918, p. 47
263 *Ibid.*, p. 61.
264 Ree Herring Hedrick, *Lineage and Tradition of the Herring, Conyers, Hendrick, Boddie, Perry Crudup, Denson and Hilliard Families*, c1916, p. 99.
265 Female Institute and Athenaeum Student Records, 1851-1853.

Jessie. On August 20, 1870, the census indicated that Jessie W. is seven months old and under the title "If born within the year, state month" is written "Nov." January 20 would have been seven months previously, and Medora was born on January 24. Is this a very serious blunder of the two children? There are no records that have been found as to the location of Medora after her mother and Dr. Peters reunited.

In the 1870 census, there were about 240 ladies ages 18 down to 9 in the convent. By the next census in 1880, Medora Peters at the age of 16 was listed among the boarding students at the Academy of the Visitation in St. Louis where Clara was a nun and teacher. In spite of this, Medora was not to follow Clara's path. After she completed her schooling, she returned to Memphis and married.[266]

Sister Mary Paula Peters was in charge of teaching music and French. For a number of years, she had entire charge of the academy's musical department. Her influence was always for good, patient, never interfering with religious vocations, but nurturing the children's spiritual life. Her rare mental and moral gifts fitted her for the difficult work of the Academy of Visitation. She had a beautiful voice and would sing any time that she was asked to perform for special musical ceremonies of the convent.[267]

For twenty years, Sister Mary Paula was Directress of the Ladies' Sodality, the Children of Mary. The Archcon fraternity of Reparation and the Ladies' Sodality were religious societies that began in the 1890s. She also saw a new gymnasium added just six years before her death. She helped those out in the world, and because of her sympathy and generous nature, she encouraged, strengthened, and uplifted everyone to higher aims. On the other hand, this was only one phase of her virtues. She was known as humble, obedient, simple and sincere, never questioning her loyalty to her Superior, and always had the interests of the community. She was known to give constant edification or instruction. It was

---
266 Shelby County, Tennessee marriage records, October 22, 1884.
267 Sisters of the Visitation, B.V.M., From our Monastery of St. Louis, Missouri, November 30, 1917.

apparent that Sister Mary Paula loved everything pertaining to the holy Order-- its spirit, its writings, its traditions, and the house in particular.[268]

Sister Josephine Barber, the last of the founding sisters, died by 1887. At that point the school was divided into senior, intermediate, and junior departments. The curriculum included catechism, math, elocution, composition, history, science, several music courses, and the required sewing, darning and calisthenics. The subjects were very similar to the Athenaeum Girls School and the Female Institute in Columbia, Tennessee, and most girls schools in the country. In 1892 the convent moved to 10 acres on Cabanne and Belt Avenues. George Barnett was the architect, and it was built to resemble a French chateau. After its completion, it was referred to as a castle in a spacious fairyland. Yearly processions to the outdoor shrine on the feast of the Sacred Heart would have as many as 2,500 attend from all over the area. The Visitation Academy remained for 70 years at that site, but in 1962, plans were begun for the current location.[269]

In 1867, Dr. Peters paid an Excise Tax to the United States Government of $655.77 on 53 bales of cotton but was raising tobacco five years later, and his taxes were only $30.

On June 13, 1872, George, Jr., married Kate Greenlaw, the daughter of John Oliver. He had just graduated from Cumberland University the year before and was already established in a law practice.[270]

Jessie had another daughter on December 23, 1871, whom she named Kate Chalmers. The house in Spring Hill was sold two years later, and they moved to Memphis. Dr. Peters held on to his property in Arkansas that enabled him to run for the state legislature in that state.[271]

During this same time, Jessie's sister Eleanor McKissack was

---

268 *Ibid.*
269 *Op. Cit.*, Watkins.
270 Shelby County, Tennessee, Marriage records, June 13, 1872.
271 *Columbia Daily Appeal*, Columbia, Tennessee, August 15, 1869.

having a great deal of serious difficulty with one her sons. On November 30, 1871, James McKissack attempted to kill his own child. Because his mother interfered, the child was saved, but James struck the mother on the head splitting her skull. Tee, a sister of James, tried to assist, and he hit her on the head penetrating the brain. Mrs. Robert I. Moore (another sister Mary Bell), also tried to assist, and she was hit in the face with a hatchet. James took a razor out of his pocket and cut his own throat, severing the windpipe.[272]

Over two years later, James went to the depot accompanied by his father to take the train for New Orleans. His trunk was put aboard and arrangements for his departure were made when he suddenly changed his mind and had his trunk removed. When his father asked about his plans being changed, James replied that he had not been furnished enough money. As soon as his father told him that he had a sufficient amount to cover his needs, James stabbed him inflicting three wounds in the chest and three in the back one of which barely missed the heart. His father fell to the ground unable to defend himself when a gentleman ran to his assistance. James started crying, "Oh, I've killed him, I've killed him." A brother intercepted James, and he was taken into custody where he remained in jail. His conduct was described as strange and unnatural and that he suffered under temporary fits of derangement.[273] An undated petition in Miscellaneous Papers in the basement of the Maury County courthouse stated that "James T. McKissack is insane and that his being at large is dangerous to the community....is in needy circumstances." It was signed by A. (Archibald ?) McKissack and Orville McKissack, Jr. James had brothers by these names.

Orville, Jr. had his own problems when charged just two months later in June with an indictment for assault with intent to kill Woodson D. Davis. He "feloniously, willfully, deliberately and maliciously attempted to kill and murder him." His bond was set at $1000, but it was reduced to $250. When the jury was chosen that

---

272 Columbia Daily Herald, Columbia, Tennessee, December 1, 1871.
273 *Nashville Union and American,* Nashville, Tennessee, April 11, 1873.

was comprised of twelve men including W. M. McKissack, they found the defendant "not guilty."[274] Woodson D. Davis and John Batchellor had purchased a lot on Market Street and built a small wooden house where they erected a blacksmith shop and stables. James W. Frierson filed a complaint in June 1841 that the premises were damaging to his property and violated the fire code. By 1870, Davis is listed as a successful farmer but was elected sheriff in 1878.[275] It is not known the circumstances of the indictment.

Orville enlisted in the Confederate army in 1864 and was one of General Nathan B. Forrest's escorts. He received a gunshot through his right knee while his unit was in Lawrence County just thirty-five miles from his home. Because inflammation set up, he was confined to his bed for about ten months. He was attended by Dr. Aaron White in whose home General Van Dorn had his first headquarters. Orville had no use of his leg and had to use crutches.[276]

It was not unusual for owners of large tracts of land to issue currency of their own. It would be given to their employees who would in turn spend it in the landowner's store. Dr. Peters issued his own currency from Peters Landing about 1873 that was also the date that Lee County was created from St. Francis, Crittenden, Monroe, and Phillips Counties. Even though most notes were printed by local printers, his notes or currency were printed by Corliss, Macy & Co. Stationers of New York. Some of the currency had a shield with the motto "In God is our Trust" that very likely came from the verse in "Star Spangled Banner." It reads, "Then conquer we must, when our cause it is just, and this be our motto, In God is our Trust."[277]

---

274 The State of Tennessee vs. Orville McKissack, Jr., Minutes of Criminal Court, Maury Co., November 17, 1874- July 1875.
275 David Peter Robbins, *Century Review 1805-1905 Maury County, Tennessee*, (Pennsylvania: Erie 1905), p. 18.
276 O. W. McKissack, Soldier's Application for Pension, June 29, 1891.
277 Suzy Keasler, *Lee County History*, (Lee County Sesquicentennial Committee: 1987), p. F248.

The Southern Claims Commission

The Southern Claims Commission was established in 1871 to give compensation to those southerners who supported the Union but had property taken by Federal troops in the area. The Commission accepted only from those who held American citizenship, resided in a state that seceded, could document loyalty to the federal government throughout the conflict, and had suffered official confiscation of goods. Dr. Peters filed a claim on April 20, 1874 in the amount of $2,050. This amount included the following: 7 mules @ $200 each, 5,000 pounds of bacon at 10¢ per pound, and one four-horse wagon for $150. Three months later, Dr. Peters had to appear before the Commissioners of Claims in Memphis for a hearing. He indicated in the petition that the supplies taken were in Coahoma County in the state of Mississippi, and he was residing there at the time. His property was taken from his plantation in Coahoma on June 2, 1863 and taken to Helena, Arkansas to be used by the troops.[278]

On October 24, six months after filing with the Southern Claims Commission, Dr. Peters and Jessie's daughter Lucy Mary died at the age of 12 just 18 days short of her birthday. She was the first to be buried in their family plot in Elmwood Cemetery in Memphis that

---

278 U. S. National Archives & Records Administration, RG 123, Cong. #3690, George B. Peters, application, tabbed, Box 484, April 22, 1876

had been established only twenty-two years by the father-in-law of Medora and some other local citizens.[279] On March 9, 1876 at their plantation in Arkansas, Jessie McKissack Peters age 38 gave birth to her last child Robert Edward Lee Peters.

A year later in May, Dr. Peters had two witnesses gave depositions in relation to the claim filed with the Southern Claims Commission. There were eighty questions that the Claims Commissioners were to ask although all of the questions did not apply to every person involved.

Martha Covington was Dr. Peters' housekeeper while her husband attended the plantation. She stated that she saw property taken that included mules, wagon, and bacon. She saw her husband talking to the officers and showing them some safe guards or protection papers that he had. The officers told him, "They are no account and he had orders from the General." They wanted the key to the smokehouse that her husband had to get from her. It was about ten o'clock in the morning when the men, some including Negroes, got off the boat, but after showing them the papers, they continued indicating that they wanted all the Negro men. She did not remember what they said about the property other than they had been ordered to take it. A gun boat stayed out in the middle of the river. They took property from four plantations that her husband attended but did not give any money or receipts. The bacon had been put up the winter before and was in the smokehouse about 20 steps from the house in which they lived. After getting the key to the smokehouse, about 50 soldiers took the bacon and carried it on their shoulders but left a great deal that was worth about 20 to 25 cents a pound.[280]

The postmaster of Memphis was Josiah DeLoach about 68 when he gave testimony in favor of Dr. Peters whom he had known since 1837. He was aware that Dr. Peters was loyal from his conversations. He also indicated that Pitser Miller (His store in Memphis was the

---

279 Memphis, Tennessee, Elmwood Cemetery records.
280 U. S. National Archives & Records Administration, RG 123, Cong. #3690, Martha E. Covington, Deposition, Box 484, April 22, 1876.

scene of Thomas Peters' death.) who was now residing in Bolivar knew that Dr. Peters was loyal; otherwise, he could not prove any actions.²⁸¹

Dr. Peters gave his testimony about the location of his plantations along with two other witnesses. He had received a Union pass to go home to Spring Hill where his family was located. He had been arrested about 50 miles below Helena, Arkansas where he had gone to buy cotton and was arrested by a Confederate soldier and taken to Meridian, Mississippi. He was there about three weeks when he was released by a writ of habeas corpus offered by some of his friends before Judge Kilpatrick. During the battle of Shiloh, he offered to amputate limbs or dress wounds of either party, but his service was not accepted. He would sometimes get a permit from Union generals including Sherman to get supplies to run his farm because his slaves preferred staying. The only time that he left his home was to hide in the island from Confederates who wanted "to break him up." General Buford at Helena wanted him to give information about some Confederate soldiers crossing that the general thought took place near his plantation, but it was 20 miles away. He told Dr. Peters to consider himself under arrest, but the general gave him a pass after the third day since he gave him all the information that he could. Supplies of a similar nature were taken from his home in June 1863 at Council Bend by General Carter.²⁸²

When General Hindman reached Little Rock on May 30, 1862, he found the command "bare of soldiers, penniless, defenseless, and dreadly exposed" to the Federal Army that was quickly approaching from the northeast.²⁸³ Three months before, the Confederate Congress had authorized the destruction of cotton, tobacco, military supplies, and other property in danger of falling in the hands of the Union Army.²⁸⁴ Dr. Peters had been threatened

---

281 *Ibid.* Josiah DeLoach.
282 *Ibid.*, George B. Peters, Deposition.
283 Diane Neal, *The Lion of the South: General Thomas C. Hindman*, (Macon, Georgia: Mercer University Press 1997), p. 119.
284 *Ibid.* p. 118.

with his life from General Hindman who ordered him to burn all the cotton that he could get. When Dr. Peters refused, the general ordered that he be hung from the nearest tree or brought to Little Rock. Servants were engaged to find out when they were coming. One night they almost caught him while he was attending a sick servant; but he escaped to the orchid where he heard what they were intending to do. He was almost caught at another time when he was fishing in Lake Mellicote but escaped from their pursuit. He did let the federals have use of what was on the plantation.

Dr. Peters told the commissioners that he had a brother and two sons who fought for the Confederacy. He got a permit from General Hurlbut to bring his wounded son to Memphis to attend to his wounds. Otherwise, he did not assist them except for $200 that relatives in Bolivar sent to his son in prison in Ft. Warren and then checked on him for the amount. He was given a pass by Van Dorn's adjutant just before shooting him. He claimed that his sympathies were always with the Union throughout the war. He had a safeguard obtained at Vicksburg from General Grant to raise a crop of cotton on Island 68, but when his man Covington at the plantation in Coahoma showed the officers, they said, "D—m the permit and tore it up." Dr. Peters also got a permit from Admiral Porter in order that his gunboats would protect him. When the Confederates found this among his papers, they took it as sufficient evidence that he was disloyal to the Confederacy and should have his property taken.[285]

Dr. Peters indicated that he was not present when his property was taken because he was in Memphis. A young pilot told him that it was General Prentiss' men who took the property. Thinking that Prentiss was an honorable man and would return the servants, Dr. Peters went to see him but was told that he would not give a permit. Since some of the servants wanted to come with him and others did not, Dr. Peters let them all stay. He went the next day to get a receipt for the mules, but Prentiss was on a raid and did not return.[286]

---

285 *Op. Cit.*, U. S. National Archives & Records Administration.
286 *Ibid.*

C. B. Clarke, son of Cleveland, was not positive concerning what was taken from the property that he identified as the Boddie place since his father's property was also taken.[287]

E. E. Clarke indicated that he was not present when the property was taken, but heard through the pilot of a steamer that his and Dr. Peters' property was taken by Captain Clammers, one of Prentiss' men. Clarke got a permit from General Hurlbut to visit Prentiss along with Dr. Peters. We told him that we were astonished that our safeguard from General Grant was violated, and he agreed. He indicated that he could not restore the men because they had already joined the army, and he was going on a raid and would have to wait about the other. Neither of them ever received supplies or receipts.[288]

On November 16, 1876, the commissioners were not satisfied as to the loyalty of Dr. Peters and asked for an investigation. The following April, a memo was sent to special agent John D. Edwards who came from Little Rock to do the investigation from Memphis.

Mrs. A. P. McNeill lived in Crittenden County, Arkansas, about two miles from Memphis. She expressed how Dr. Peters and often his wife were always stopping at their house and staying overnight on their way to Memphis. Sometimes, she would accompany them into Memphis, but this was at the beginning of the war when the Confederates occupied Memphis. She believed that Dr. Peters was as strong a southern man as her husband. They were always agreeing with each other, and she saw Dr. Peters three or four times before Memphis was occupied by the Federals. She claimed that those she knew always regarded Dr. Peters as a grand southern man. She knew that many southern men made pretenses to go among the federals to get supplies when all the time they were in favor of the south.[289]

Fielding Hurst was an attorney who lived in McNairy County

---

287 *Ibid.*, C. B. Clarke, Deposition.
288 Ibid., Edwards E. Clarke, Deposition as to Property.
289 *Ibid.*, Deposition as to Loyalty.

next to Hardeman County, Tennessee all of his adult life and was well acquainted with all the prominent men in the area. He was loyal to the U. S. government and served in the 6th Tennessee U. S. Cavalry. He knew Dr. Peters because he had made the canvass as a Breckenridge Democrat in 1860. They had conversations immediately prior to the breaking out of the war, and Hurst claimed Dr. Peters was always an avowed secessionist of the extreme order. He was an open rebel up to the time of his killing Van Dorn. He left Bolivar with a Confederate company and remained with the Confederates until he killed Van Dorn after which he came into the federal lines[290]

Josiah DeLoach again related that he had seen Dr. Peters often, but could not specify any occasion when he discussed support of the Union except when he returned from the Tennessee legislature and was the only man who stood up against succession. He could not remember one word that was said in favor of the Federal Government during the war or any actions, but Dr. Peters was always regarded as a Union man.[291]

Edwards Clark was a commission merchant in Memphis and first met Dr. Peters four years before the war. He had a plantation less than three miles from Dr. Peters' place in Mississippi. He admitted that he supported the Union, and therefore, conversed with Dr. Peters very often sometimes two or three times a week and then sometimes not for two weeks, but he was always a strong Union man. He claimed that Dr. Peters stated that we were all ruined, and slavery was at an end. There was no reason for the war, and he was the only one in the Tennessee Senate who objected to vote in the secession question. He believed that if Jefferson Davis were made president of the southern states that it would not stand for two months. Clark related how he went with Dr. Peters to see the quartermaster of General Sherman and introducing him. He knew that publicly Dr. Peters was known as being loyal to the

---

290 *Ibid.*
291 *Ibid.*, Josiah DeLoach, Deposition as to Loyalty.

Union, but he did not know if any money or aid was given to the Union cause. He knew that Dr. Peters took the oath of allegiance and talked to others. Clark was asked, "Did not the claimant leave Memphis with the Confederate army and keep out of the Federal lines until after the killing of Van Dorn?" Clark responded that he did not see Dr. Peters in Memphis at that time and did not know whether he did or not.[292]

When Dr. Peters was asked if he had ever had Confederate passes, he responded only one two days before he killed Van Dorn to go to Nashville. Van Dorn gave him the pass to get rid of him. Dr. Peters indicated that he did not want to speak about the incident, but he could not explain the matter otherwise. He was pursued to Shelbyville where his friend Major J. J. Murphy gave him a pass indicating that he was going to Kentucky for coffee and sugar for the officers.

He repeated a great deal of the information that he had given before; however, the deposition was more in depth. He told about being arrested for the Van Dorn matter. He had previously given little reference to his killing General Van Dorn, and it was still limited. He had purchased some cotton in different areas and obtained a pass from Union General Buford to go to Eldorado, Arkansas to take a few articles to his mother. He emphasized how he told his two sons that it was a mistake to fight for the Confederacy because they were "bound to be whipped." When asked if his sympathies were with the federal government or people of the South, Dr. Peters stated that the U. S. government should maintain it supremacy over these states, but he had sympathy for those by whom he was surrounded. When asked if he assisted his sons, he stated that he sent his son Arthur $200 while he was in prison in Ft. Warren. When Thomas enlisted, he was 19, and he did give him some clothes and more when he came home wounded.[293]

Cleveland B. Clarke was commission merchant and a brother

---

292 *Ibid.*, Edwards E. Clarke, Deposition of Loyalty.
293 *Ibid.*, George B. Peters, Deposition.

to Edwards. He was too young to remember any details about his father and Dr. Peters' property being taken in the summer of 1863. He remembered that individuals around them would curse Dr. Peters as supporting the Yankees. Cleveland knew that his father was loyal to the U.S. government, and that he talked freely to Dr. Peters about the matter. He did remember that a gunboat stopped at a place near them and officers got a quantity of cotton that Dr. Peters had hidden in the bushes prior to its being shipped to Memphis. Cleveland went to the officers and told them about a safeguard from General Grant in the possession of Dr. Peters if they wished for him to go and get it. About three times guards asked about Dr. Peters because they wanted to catch him. They were very isolated in the area were their property was located and their neighbors were very disloyal. He had often heard Dr. Peters express that the Union was a good one. He had heard persons refer to Dr. Peters as a d---d Yankee. It was because he was selling cotton and buying supplies.[294]

Cleveland Clarke reported that he was going to his father's plantation when he encountered soldiers taking property. They said that they had already stripped Dr. Peters. Cleveland told them that they had a safeguard from General Grant and presented the papers. He was told that it was too late; when at the moment, he pointed out the clause that indicated that a violation of this is death. The officer stated that he left the responsibility with his commanding officer General Prentiss[295]

Ferdinand B. Montana was a steamboat pilot and captain who had known Dr. Peters about 30 years. Before and since the war, he often traveled on his boat. Montana considered him a Confederate as a matter of course. He understood that Dr. Peters was on one of the regiments of General Van Dorn's command in the quarter masters department; however, it was from hearsay and general notoriety. He understood that his brother was a quartermaster and stationed in

---

294 *Ibid.*, Cleveland B. Clarke, Deposition as to loyalty.
295 *Ibid.*, Cleveland B. Clarke, Deposition as to Property.

Memphis. After the trouble with Van Dorn, he came back in Federal lines. Montana engaged in the cotton business and sympathized with the South. It would be difficult for any man suspected of being a Union man to go outside the Union lines without being in danger. He saw Dr. Peters only two or three times during the war and knew of only one or two acres cultivated on Island 68 during the war other than a wood yard for steamboats.[296]

One of the witnesses was Lee Clark, a former slave, who continued to live on Cleveland B. Clark's plantation adjoining Dr. Peters. He claimed that when he went to the Clarke boat landing, he saw four of Dr. Peters' mules already on the boat.[297]

Dr. Peters' petition for the reimbursement of the supplies taken from one of his plantations was questioned from the beginning. The commissioners were not satisfied and requested that a government agent be sent for the purpose of investigating his loyalty and the claim.[298]

Special Agent John D. Edwards went to Memphis and the vicinity during May and June 1877 and reviewed all of the evidence and the witnesses. Dr. Peters was questioned again that included a great deal about his time in the Tennessee Senate. He stated that when the Ordinance of Secession was submitted to the people in 1861, he was the only senator who did not vote for it the day that it passed. Although he was in Nashville, he would not go and vote. He indicated that there were four senators who voted against submitting it to the people although he thought all were going to vote for it. Senator Stockly, who the day before had voted against the proposition changed his vote. Then Dr. Peters had his vote recorded in the same way because some of them were Union men. In February, 60,000 people voted against, and they thought it would happen again.

Agent Edwards asked the following question:

---

[296] *Ibid.*, Ferdinard B. Montana, Deposition as to loyalty.
[297] *Ibid.*, Lee Clarke , Deposition as to loyalty.
[298] *Ibid.*, Abstract for Agent.

Did you not then state in the presence of Spl. Agt. Edwards and Spl. Comm. Dix that the next morning after the vote had been taken you went down to the Senate and that the clerk to the Senate asked you to allow your vote to be recorded in favor of the article and that you refused to allow it to be done and was not this offer your deposition had been closed when you and the men talking in a general way and did not one of them ask you if you wanted that in your deposition and did you not reply that you did not care about it. Is not that about the way it all took place at the time your mention about two months ago.

Dr. Peters indicated that the clerk asked him to do, and he responded that he should vote against it. Four refused to let him record it that I voted for it the day that it passes, but after consulting with some of his friends, he had his vote recorded. He then said that he had not been contacted or received any information about the proceedings, but had tried to get a copy. He continued to discuss the conversation with the clerk who told him that he would be ruined if he did not vote for succession. Dr. Peters refused until he discussed it with others.[299]

John D. Edwards wrote seven legal size pages in an abstract of the evidence:

Witnesses Examined

<u>Geo. B. Peters</u> Claimant does not appear like a man of very sound mind, his evidence in regard to his vote on the Ordinance of Secession while a member of the Tennessee Senate will show that there is little confidence to be placed in his statements.

<u>Josiah DeLoach</u> Late postmaster at Memphis, his only claim to be considered loyal is founded on the fact that he once warned a party of officers who had come to his house to get something to eat, that the guerrillas would catch them if they stayed there; his motive in this was possibly

---

299 *Ibid.*, George B. Peters Deposition before Special Agent John D. Edwards.

to keep his premises free from a skirmish, but as the party consisted of Gen. Grant and his staff, it turned out to be a very advantageous warning to witness. DeLoach is said to have been at Shiloh or Pittsburg Landing with the rebel forces, and passed as a good Confederate in the early part of the war; he is a simple farmer, of not much mind, but considerable kindness of heart, and seems to have been willing to testify to the loyalty of nearly everybody who asked him to vouch for them, in the present case he lived 40 or 50 miles from claimant, did not see him more than two or three times during the war, and practically knows nothing about him.

Edwards E. Clarke Is a claimant himself, and Peters is one of his witnesses. Looks very unfavorable, and manner while under examination, such as to excite doubt as the truth of his evidence, he bears the reputation in Memphis of being a sharp business man, not over scrupulous as to the means employed to accomplish his ends.

Cleveland B. Clarke. Appears to resemble his father, was, at a recent term of court placed under bond to answer indictment to be preferred against him for alleged complicity in the murder of one M. M. Beach a sewing machine agent, by his (Clarke's brother-in-law) one Coe.

Ferdinand B. Montana-47 Steamboat captain and pilot, appears of a frank and open disposition, is probably to be relied on where not personally interested, was a rebel in sympathy during the war.

Lee Clarke (Cold) Former slave of Edwards & Clarke and still living on Clarkes place, will probably say whatever Clarke tells him to.

Mrs. A. P. McNeill. A lady who lived on the river in Crittenden Co. Ark., about half way between Memphis, and the claimants house, appeared to tell the truth as far as she knew it, had no idea she was to be examined in the case until she was called on by the agent.

Fielding Hurst-66 Was Col. of 6th Tenn. Vols. U.S.A. is a man of decided opinion, and strong expression thereof, but is a gentleman, and much valiance may be place in his statements.

LINDA GUPTON

Evidence in favor of loyalty

Josiah DeLoach Can't recollect any word or act of the claimants, but refers to his former deposition when the matter was fresher in his mind. i.e. remembers well for 12 years, but can't recollect for 14 years.

Edwards E. Clarke Spent a good deal of time with claimant, who always talked as a Union man. Claimant took the oath of allegiance, and talked to others, as he did to the witness. Don't know whether claimant left Memphis with rebel army or not, don't remember seeing him after rebel army left Memphis, up to time he killed Van Dorn.

Geo. B. Peters-62 Desired that the Federal Government should maintain supremacy, but sympathized with his people, told his sons before they went in the rebel that it was a great mistake, the South was bound to be whipped, and they should stay of the army.

Cleveland B. Clarke was too young to be entrusted with much, but heard the people curse claimant and speak of him as a d-d Yankee. Claimant and witness father were the only ones about there who could get their cotton out, and get supplies. claimant could not visit his plantation part of the time without keeping "hid out." Don't know of any act of claimant showing him friendly to the U. S. except shipping cotton inside the Federal lines. People down there spoke of claimant as a friend of he government because he sold cotton inside the lines.

Evidence against loyalty

Josiah DeLoach Does not know of claimant doing anything to prevent him from proving loyalty to the Confederacy.

Edwards E. Clarke Does not remember seeing claimant in Memphis from the time it was evacuated by the rebels, till after the time he killed Van Dorn. According to the evidence he witness own case he moved to N. Y. with his family in 1863 so that his opportunities for seeing and observing claimant could not have been very extended.

George B. Peters Claimant killed Rebel Genl. Van Dorn

in May 1863 on account of a personal matter, went down into the Confederacy after that, was arrested on account of Van Dorn affair, and taken before Gen. Johnson, who decided that as the claimant did not belong to the army, he could only be tried by the civil courts, this was surely extradinary forbearance, and shows that Peters must have proved himself a rebel beyond all doubt; or they would have put an end to him, then, and there; to justify this view still further it may be noted that claimant afterwards went to Atlanta, and there gave bond to Isham G. Harris of Tenn. to appear at the first court after the war. This Harris was the "War Governor" of Tenn. and was the most ultra rebel in the Confederacy now it is an impossibility that Harris would have done such a favor to help a loyal man who had killed a favorite rebel general, but claimant must himself have been so sound a Confederate that even a crime so heinous in Confederate eyes was condoned by Peters own record.

In a supplemental deposition given by the claimant he qualifies his statement as to being the only senator who did not vote for the ordinance of secession, although in a conversation with the Agent before Spec. Com. Dix, he had so asserted, he admits that the day after the vote had been taken he had his vote recorded in favor of the ordinance of secession 1st May 1861. Admits that he gave the Agent & Mr. Dix to believe the other way. (probably heard that Agent had got hold of the Senate Journal)

<u>Ferdinand B. Montana</u> Claimant was on the Confederate side, heard he was in the rebel army, and did not see him about Memphis for a long time. Witness was engaged in the cotton business, and knows that no man, who was suspected of being loyal to U.S. could go outside the lines, and trade in cotton, without being in danger. Did not know that claimant had a place near Island No. 68 during the war, his place was at Council Bend, 40 miles below Memphis, there was only two or three acres cultivated at Island 68 that was by the man who kept cord wood there for steamboats.

<u>Mrs. A. P. McNeill</u> was well acquainted with claimant, witness lived about halfway between Dr. Peters and Memphis, and claimant frequently stopped at their house overnight on his way to and from Memphis, during the early months of

the war, witness frequently went to Memphis with claimant & his wife, witness believed from what claimant said, that he was a strong Southern man, frequently heard her husband and claimant talk together on the subject, always regarded claimant as a southern man, and he was looked on that way by those who knew him.

<u>Col, Fielding Hurst</u> was well acquainted with the claimant, they were young men together in Hardeman County, Tenn. Saw him several times in 1861. Claimant in 1860 made the canvass as a Breckenridge Democrat in conversation with witness before the breaking out of the war. Claimant was always an avowed secessionist of the extreme order. Claimant was an open rebel up to the time he killed Van Dorn. Claimant left Bolivar with the Confederates, and remained in their lines till he killed Van Dorn, then he came into the Federal lines.

Record evidence from Senate Journal

<u>Page 15</u>. April 26th 1861. "Mr. Minnis introduced Senate Bill No. 1 to submit to a vote of the people an ordinance dissolving their connection with the General Government which passed its first reading." This Senate Bill No 1. was known as the Tennessee Ordinance of Secession.

<u>Page 29</u>. April 30th. Senate Bill No 1 taken up on third reading.

<u>Page 33.</u> April 30th 1861. Senate Bill No. 1. Passed with only 4 nays, to wit; Messrs, Boyd, Nash, Stokely & Trimble.

<u>Page 35.</u> May 1st, 1861. Geo. B. Peters, Senator from counties of Hardin, McNairy, and Hardeman appeared and took his seat "this seems to be claimants first appearance this session." Mr. Peters asked and obtained leave to record his vote in the affirmative upon the passage of Senate Bill No. 1" & c.

<u>Page 39.</u> May 2nd 1861. Senate Resolution No. 20, is offered requesting senators in Congress to resign seats as U.S. government had become a military despotism.

<u>Pages 41 & 42.</u> May 2, 1861. Claimant moves to amend "bill to raise, organize & equip provisional force."

Page 46. May 3, 1861. Claimant votes in favor of Senate Resolution No. 20, requesting Senators in U.S. Congress to resign seats.

Page 53-5. May 4th, 1861. Claimant moves that his amendments to bill to raise, organize, and equip provisional force be rejected, and finally votes in favor of bill.

Pages 67 to 69. May 7th, 1861. Claimant votes yea on Senate Resolution No. 31. That the State of Tennessee form offensive and defensive league with Confederate States of America.

Pages 107 & 108. June 19th, 1861. Claimant votes yea on Senate Resolution No. 40. "The People of Tennessee have dissolved political relation with the government of U.S." &c

Page 109. June 19th 1861. Claimant introduces Senate Resolution No. 41, Calling for information on artillery service of state.

Page 123. June 22nd, 1861. claimant votes yea on Senate Bill No. 12. Also makes motion in regard to pay of private soldiers in Tenn. Vol. Troops.

Page 156 & 158. June 28th, 1861. Claimant votes yea, on House Bills 31 & 39 Regulations for military companies.

Page 178. June 29th, 1861. Claimant votes on House resolution No. 70. Location of Capitol of Confederate States.

Conclusion

There is no definite evidence to the taking of property, Mrs. Covington who said to have been the only eye witness produced by the claimant is said to be dead.

According to the evidence the property was taken at the same time it is alleged that Edwards E. Clark (Claim No. 1204) had property taken from the adjoining place by the U.S. Troops. Information obtained in Clarke's case points to the fact that the corn and meat taken there was rebel army supplies, and not private property—as these two plantations were adjoining, and there is really no evidence to be had as to where the property was-this-together with the prevarication and disingenuousness of claimant in his evidence about his loyalty throws doubt on the whole matter, and gives ground for the belief that the claim is groundless both as regards loyalty and property

Respectfully submitted
John D. Edwards
Special Agent

Hon. Commissioners of Claims
Washington, D.C.

The first of December 1877, the Commissioners of Claims disallowed Dr. Peters' claim. In their statement, they indicated that Dr. Peters gave testimony that he was the only one voting against succession when in fact there were four. He furnished only opinions of partial witnesses in support of loyalty and did nothing tangible in conduct or expression. They regarded him as having been unquestionably disloyal; and, therefore, rejected the claim.[300]

Dr. Peters filed another petition with the Court of Claims. He stated that he was loyal and the decision was unjust. Gilbert Moyers of Washington, D. C. was hired as his attorney on April 25, 1888. Dr. Peters died a year later on April 29, 1889.

In a letter to the Attorney General dated October 15, 1892, the Treasury Department acting secretary sent the following letter:

> In answer to your request of the 28th ultimo, in the case of Geo. B. Peters, No. 3640 Congressional, I have the honor to transmit herewith, duly authenticated, under the seal of this Department, a copy of the official bond of a Brigade Quartermaster of the army, C.S.A., on which the name of Geo. B. Peters appears as one of the sureties, from the Confederate Archives in the possession of this Department, (Office No. 31, P.)

The first paragraph of the sheet with the title was stated:

CONFEDERATE STATES OF AMERICA

KNOW ALL MEN BY THESE PRESENTS, That I Thomas Peters of the State of Tennessee as principal, and George B.

---

[300] *Ibid.,*, Special Agent John D. Edwards' Report.

Peters, Wm. G. Ford, R. C. Brinkley, W. J. Davie and J. J. Murphy, of the State of Tennessee as sureties, are held and firmly bound unto the <u>Confederate States of America</u>, in the full and just sum of Thirty Thousand Dollars, to the payment whereof, well and truly to be made, we bind ourselves, jointly and severally, our joint and several heirs, executors and administrators, firmly by these present.

The rest of the legal obligation dated November 25, 1861 in Memphis was for the appointment of Thomas Peters to the office of Brigade Quarter Master in the Provisional Army of the Confederate States of America as an official bond to fully execute his duties. It was approved in January by Judah P. Benjamin, Secretary of War.[301]

Dr. Peters died in 1889 never knowing that the Treasury Department's report on loyalty had been discovered. It was written proof of his support in part of the war although it was for his brother. The J. J. Murphy, who also signed as one of the sureties, was his friend whom he had listed in his disposition as giving him a pass in Shelbyville shortly after Van Dorn's death.

---

301 *Ibid.*,U.S.A. Treasury Department Report on loyalty, Deposition, Box 484,October 15, 1892.

Dr. Peters' Last Years

Dr. Peters was a part of the Tennessee legislature as the state was preparing for war. He was elected to represent Phillips and Lee counties of Arkansas on September 1, 1884, and would be dealing with many issues that had been caused by the same war. Over a month later, Medora would marry Henry Lenow and live in Memphis.

After finishing her schooling in St. Louis at the Academy of Visitation, Medora returned to Memphis. She met Henry Lenow, who was from a prosperous family in the Shelby County area. His father was Captain Joseph Lenow, who received his rank in the Mexican War. In 1837 he emigrated from Southampton County, Virginia to Fayette County in Tennessee. He was successful in the mercantile pursuits but moved to Memphis eleven years later. He laid the foundation of many successful business interests that included real estate, president of Branch Bank of Tennessee, director of the Mississippi and Tennessee Railroad for 12 years, and 31 years as president of the company that established Elmwood Cemetery in 1852.[302] He was known for sending his ten year old son and a black boy by the name of Majordome through Federal lines while he drove an old buggy with quinine and lint dressing in the spokes to

---

302 "Death of Joseph Lenow-The Father of Elmwood Passes to His Grave," *Commercial Appeal*, Memphis, Tennessee, September 20, 1889.

the Confederate troops. These same two boys were known to have placed the same powder in the carcass of a dead horse that they were allowed to drag through the Federal lines to the waiting rebels.[303]

Henry Lenow was a cashier in his father's bank and continued to work in the bank after he and Medora married on October 22, 1884. In later years, he was the president of the German-American Bank. The couple had fifteen children, and other than the daughter that they lost in 1899 and Louise in 1901, Henry and Medora were fortunate not to lose a son during the Great War. They were constantly concerned about their daughter Lucy, who suffered from epilepsy.[304]

The 25th General Assembly of Arkansas convened on January 25, 1885, and lasted three months. During this time, the Act of April 6, 1869, was repealed that provided for funding for Railroad Aid. In this manner nearly $14 million of a debt of $17 million, the greater part of which had been "saddled" on the state of carpetbag government of the Clayton regime, was eliminated. They created a state debt board composed of the governor, auditor, treasurer, and attorney general who would handle payment of the balance of the bonded indebtedness. The board would determine which bonds were legal and genuine and report to the next General Assembly. Other decisions included changing the name of Dorsey County to Cleveland, better protection of fish and game, and appropriated $5000 to defray the expenses of the Arkansas exhibit at the Cotton Centennial Exposition in New Orleans.[305]

Just a month after the 25th General Assembly first session ended, William Peters, the first child of Jessie and Dr. Peters to reach adulthood, died on April 6, 1885, at the age of 25. He had been a merchant at Council Bend that had probably been the store

---

303 *History of Homes and Gardens of Tennessee*, (Nashville, Tennessee: The Garden Study Club), p. 318.
304 Interview with Laura W. Walker, Granddaughter of Medora Peters Lenow, Memphis, Tennessee, August 2009.
305 Arkansas Legislature General Assembly, January 25, 1885 to March 28, 1885.

that belonged to his father. He was buried in Memphis' Elmwood Cemetery in the family plot next to his sister Lucy.

Dr. Peters was elected on September 6, 1886. The 26th Assembly that began the following January appropriated over 1.8 million dollars for free schools. They erected buildings for the Deaf Mute Institute, School for the Blind, a lunatic asylum, two buildings for the penitentiary, and repaired and improved the capital building. No passes by railroad or transportation companies were to be given to any officers or employees of the state. Public executions were abolished, a geological survey was to be done for the state, and there was to be no intoxicating sale of liquor within three miles of schools.[306] Dr. Peters finished the session and was encouraged to run for the Congress of the United States, but he refused to allow his name to be nominated.[307]

He must have realized his health was declining because he died at the age of 74 on Monday morning of April 29, 1889, in the home of Medora. By this time she had a daughter Helene Jessie age 3, a son Francis Jesep age 3 months, and Lila would be born in 6 months. The funeral was held in Medora's home at 18 Walker Avenue at 10:00 am the next day.[308] As Jessie was preparing for the funeral, she was putting on the traditional mourning black and said, "Well, I never cared for George, but I guess I owe him this much." He was buried in Elmwood Cemetery with his children by Jessie.[309]

Dr. Peters had written his will just two months before his death. It was admitted to probate and recorded on the day that he was buried. It contained the following:

Last Will and Testament of
George B. Peters

---

306 Arkansas Legislature General Assembly, January 10, 1887.

307 Suzy Keasler, *Lee County History*, (Lee County Sesquicentennial Committee: 1987), p. F248.

308 "Death of Geo. B. Peters," *Commercial Appeal*, Memphis, Tennessee, April 30, 1889.

309 "The Mysteries of Spring Hill, Tennessee," *Blue & Gray Magazine*, Vol. II, Issue 2, Columbus, Ohio, p. 19.

I, George B. Peters, being of sound mind and memory so hereby make this as my last will and testament, revoking any and all wills which may have been heretofore by me made—that is to say:

Item 1. I will and direct that all of my just debts shall be paid by my executor as soon as practicable after my death.

Item 2. I give and bequeath to my wife, Jessie H. Peters, all of my household furniture of every kind and description now in my residence at Gill Station the title to said residence property having already by my direction been vested in her.

Item 3. I have already disposed of my real estate as follows: I have sold what is known as my Home Place in Lee county, Arkansas to my son James A. Peters, with all the personalty thereon. I have sold the place known as the Peters Island Place in Tunica County, Mississippi, and all the personalty thereon, to my son George B. Peters, Jr. I have made deeds of gift to my daughter Dora Lenow (wife of Henry Lenow) of the places known as the Kittrell and Blanford places in Crittenden County, Arkansas; a similar deed to my daughter, Kate C. Peters, of the place known as the Cook Place in Lee County, Arkansas; and a deed of gift also to my son Robert Lee Peters of the place in Lee county, Arkansas, known as my "Mound Place"—these three deeds of gift being made subject to a five years lease, J. F. Hodges being a tenant of the Kittrell and Blanford places, and Lee Webster, of the Cook and Mound places, under said leases for said period of five years, and the rent notes due by said tenants for the rent of said places being retained by me under said deeds of gift.

Item 4 I appoint my son James A. Peters, of Lee County, Arkansas, Executor of this will, and of my Estate; and direct that he shall not be required to give any bond as such Executor, as I have the utmost confidence in his capacity and integrity. Should my son J. A. Peters die before the final settlement of my Estate, I appoint in that event my son George B. Peters, Jr. as my Executor—he to serve upon the same terms, and with the same powers and duties prescribed herein as to my son James A. Peters.

Item 5 I do further appoint my said son James A. Peters, and my wife Jessie H. Peters, as guardians to act jointly, of my daughter Kate C. Peters, and of my son Robert Lee Peters, both of whom are minors.

They shall not be required to execute any bond as guardians, being hereby expressly excused therefrom. In the event of the death of either of them, or of the failure of them to serve as guardians, the other shall have the same powers and rights as are hereby conferred on the two jointly, and in the event of the death of both of the guardians herein appointed, or a refusal to serve, before Kate C. and Robert Lee Peters both come of age, I hereby appoint, in order to avoid a vacancy in the guardianship, my son George B. Peters, Jr. and my son-in-law Henry Lenow as guardians of the said children—they to serve upon the same terms, and with the same powers, duties and rights as are prescribed herein with regard to the guardians first named. The guardians shall take charge and control of the property conveyed by me to said minor children; and, after the expiration of the leases thereon herein before mentioned, shall manage and control the same, and rent out or operate the plantation as they may deem best, and invest, in their best judgment, and surplus proceeds of the same over and above the personal expenditures of said minors respectively as they may deem proper.

The Guardianship of said children shall continue until said Kate C. Peters, and Robert Lee Peters shall respectively arrive at twenty-one years of age; and that if Robert Lee Peters shall continue longer if deemed necessary by his mother, as provided in the deed to him.

Item 6 I will and direct that my executor shall out of any funds on hand at the time of my death pay my funeral expenses and all of just debts; and if there is a residue left after paying these, he shall pay over the same to my wife, Jessie H. Peters. My Executor is also authorized to settle and compromise any of my debts.

Item 7 The deeds of gift to my children herein before referred to have been signed and acknowledged by me, but are not yet recorded, except the one to my daughter Dora Lenow; and I direct my Executor to put them on record immediately upon my death should I not record them before then.

The words in item 5 "his mother as provided in the deed to him" were interlined by before signing.

In Witness whereof, I hereby sign, make, publish, and declare the above—that is, this and the foregoing four pages—to be my last will and testament.

This February 21st, 1889.

Geo. B. Peters

After the War, James went to Council Bend, Arkansas, where his father had large land holdings located on the Mississippi River 25 miles northeast of Marianna near the community of Hughes and about the same distance southwest of Memphis. The area was named for the first person who built a house in that locality, and at one time was a boat landing on the Mississippi River. It was located in part of Crittenden County just past Memphis, but in 1873, Lee County was developed out of Phillips, St. Francis, Crittenden, and Monroe Counties.

The area became Peters Mound, Peters Island, or Peters Landing after James Arthur Peters began living there. Lieut. Dabney M. Scales served on the CSA Atlanta with James during the War and knew him very well. He described James as a true gentleman, always reliable, and noted for his application to duty, and a frank generous nature. He rarely went to Memphis and led the life of a recluse, having never married, as he occupied himself looking after his plantation and spending his leisure hours in reading.

On Monday, January 31, 1891, at the age of 46, James Arthur Peters died at his home in Council Bend. The Memphis *Public Ledger* printed a telegram from Helena, Arkansas, stating that "Mr. Peters committed suicide on account of business troubles." Those who knew James said that this was not true. His death was caused by an overdose of morphine that he had taken for bilious colic.

He had suffered a great deal and was not able to get a doctor and, therefore, took the morphine to relieve the pain. When it was too late to save him, the attendants realized that he had taken an overdose.[310] Opium is obtained from the opium poppy by scraping the unripe seed capsule, collecting, and then drying the rubbery exudates. It is also the source of morphine and heroin. Morphine was known as laudanum in the 1800s and was popular and available in groceries and markets. It was one of the most powerful analgesics known and acts as an anesthetic without decreasing consciousness. A side effect is a feeling of detachment from the world along with euphoria and sometimes pleasure. It suppresses the respiratory system and high doses are fatal by respiratory failure. Even an ordinary medical dose of morphine taken with alcohol can prove deadly. Just a little over three weeks before, James bought from Mansfield Drug Company, Importers and Wholesale Druggists in Memphis the following:

3 Bottles	$39.65 Gallon	Kentucky Club Whiskey	118.95
1.5	42.92	Lynnwood Whiskey	64.38
1.10	44.00	Gin	48.40
.5	5.00	Qt. Flasks	2.50
.5	3.25	½ qt. Flasks	1.63
5	.15	Corks	.75
		Delivery	.50
			237.11[311]

Just six years later, the *Commercial Appeal* was reporting that cocaine habits were spreading so rapidly in Memphis that two drug stores were remaining open all night to accommodate the traffic in this dangerous drug. They indicated that its use was first confined to Negro women, but it had now spread to many white and black roustabouts on the steamboats. The claims were that it enables them

---

310 Death of Arthur Peters," *The Appeal-Avalanche*, Memphis, Tennessee, February 2. 1891.

311 Receipt from Mansfield Drug Company Importers and Wholesale Druggists, Estate records of James A. Peters, Marianna, Arkansas, January 8, 1891.

to stand long watches without falling asleep, and for this reason, many with the morphine habits had switched to cocaine. The drug was usually sold in a very fine powder that was sniffed through the nostril. White women fearful of damaging the contour of their noses, dissolved the powder in water and injected it hypodermically that was developed about 1850. A confirmed user would spend about a dollar a day on the drug and would steal or beg because the habit dominated their reason. Often Negro washerwomen or maids would buy a dime's worth of cocaine to strengthen themselves for a particularly hard day in their employer's home. By the turn of the century, the seriousness of the problem became apparent and regulations began to be passed. Facilities were established to assist those who became addicted.[312]

The next day after his death, James' remains were taken by his brother State Attorney General George B. Peters to his home in Memphis where funeral services were held. The next day his brother and other friends came with the train bearing his body to his boyhood home in Bolivar, Tennessee. Funeral services were held at St. James Episcopal Church where his brother Thomas had been twenty-five years earlier and buried in Polk Cemetery.[313]

James had written the following will eleven years earlier:

> Know all men by these present that of Jas. A. Peters of Lee County Arkansas do make and publish this as my last will and testament, hereby revoking any will that may by me heretofore have been made--
>
> I will and direct that my funeral expenses and all of my just debts shall be paid as speedily as possible after my death.
>
> I do give, devise, deed bequeath unto the children of my brother George B. Peters, Jr. all of my property of every description, real, personal and mixed—the same to go to his male children, if any are born lately in few simple, and to his female children absolutely in fee simple, also, but

---

[312] *Commercial Appeal*, Memphis, Tennessee, October 24, 1897.
[313] *Memphis Public Ledger*, Memphis, Tennessee, February 2, 1891.

they or each of them, to hold the same to their or her sole and separate use, free from the debts, contracts, control or liabilities of any husband they or any of them may have--

I will and direct that my Executors or the survivors of them, thereafter named shall have the power and authority to manage and control and make contracts concerning any real or personal property herein devised or bequeathed belonging to any minor child of my said brother George B. Peters, Jr. in such manner as to them may seem best and proper but they are given no authority to bind such property by their contracts and they or the survivors of them are required to make report to the proper court in Arkansas of their dealings about said minors property—

I hereby nominate and appoint my brother George B. Peters, Jr. and my father George B. Peters (and the survivor of them shall have power to act) as Executors of this my last will and testament—

But as I have full confidence in their integrity I expressly declare that they shall not be required to give any bond as Executors or to carry out the provisions of this will.

In witness whereof I have herewith set my hand and seal this fourteen (14th) day of February 1880.

Attest   Luke W. Finlay   seal   J. A. Peters
          W. P. Wilson

This instrument was signed in our presence by Jas. A. Peters and in the presence of both us and he is specially called our attention thereto and acknowledged to us both that he executed the same for the purposes therein contained and setforth and as his last will and testament—

W. P. Wilson   Luke W. Finlay
Deposing witness   Deposing witness

James had not paid his taxes on 640 acres valued at $4000. By the time the state general, state sinking fund, state school, county general and debt, district school, towns of Marianna and Haynes, the bill was $280. The appraisers gave the following of his personal property:

1 clock	$25.00
1 desk	5.00
1 silver watch	10.00
Library	25.00
2 beds &bedding	12.00
6 dining chairs	.60
1 arm chair	.50
1 clock	1.00
1 burcan	5.00
8 bottom planters	8.00
3 hang pots	3.00
6 pony plows	9.00
2 old mirrors	7.50
2 cows and calves	2.00
1 light bay horse	50.00

Mules:

Scott	75.00
Mobile	25.00
Satch	50.00
Sam	40.00
Bell	50.00
Ida	75.00
Rock	75.00
Nancy	15.00
Kity	40.00
Rayfield	15.00
Emma	75.00
Charlie	65.00
1 lot vise anvil and bellows	7.50
1 wagon	10.00

bed and bedding	$10.00
1 gold watch	30.00
1 book case	7.00
1 round table	1.00
1 single bed and bedding	3.00
2 shot guns	6.00
1 rifle	3.00
6 trunks	12.00

1 washstand	1.00
1 cooking stove & utensil	3.00
1 broken lot Blacksmith tools	1.50
13 combination Avery stocks	9.65
2 one horse cultivators	2.00
1 sorrel horse	50.00
1 dining table and dishes	5.00
Cairo	65.00
Button	10.00
Bill	50.00
Joe	35.00
Ada	80.00
Bob	75.00
Ella	15.00
Daisy	30.00
Cora	50.00
Scott No. 2	25.00
Kate	75.00
Alax	75.00
2 others	35.00
Plow tools	25.00
Farm bell	15.00

Everything had to be sold to satisfy James' debts. Although his will indicated that his debts were to be paid as quickly as possible after his death, they were not settled until well into six years later. Some of his land was sold on the courthouse steps to settle the estate. His sister-in-law Katie B. Peters bought two of the tracts of land for $286.[315]

Kate Chalmers was 16 and Robert Edward Lee was 13 when

---

[314] J. A Peters Estate Records, Marianna, Arkansas, Affidavit of Appraisers, November 16, 1891.

[315] J. A. Peters Estate Records, Lee Probate Court, Report of Sale, Marianna, Arkansas, August 1896.

their father died. Along with Jessie, they continued to live in their fashionable house at 1533 McLemore Street in Memphis. Medora had 15 children over a 22 year period losing two daughters shortly after they were born.

Dr. Peters appointed James Arthur as executor of his will and joint guardian with Jessie of his minor children. No one could comprehend that Arthur would die less than two years later by an overdose of morphine. He was in serious financial difficulties and everything had to be sold causing the estate to drag on for several years.

Jessie's Last Years With Her Family

Kate attended a girls school in Memphis and later a finishing school in Baltimore, Maryland. She returned to Memphis to marry Ezra Wallace Holden on April 17, 1895. He was born in Ohio but grew up in New Jersey. His family moved to Memphis where his youngest brother was born and their father was an agent for the Reading Pennsylvania Dispatch. While they were living in Memphis, he was manager of a cement company.[316] Four years later their only child William Robert was born. There were apparently difficulties in the marriage because Kate filed for divorce after six years. She met in court on July 29, 1901, but Ezra did not appear to defend himself. Necessary publications were completed and properly made, and he admitted to allegations that were stated. Kate and her child were living with Jessie and had been for more than two years. The divorce papers specified that they were able to maintain the child, and the father had failed and neglected to provide and support them. He had abandoned them for more than two years. The child was given to Kate, but Ezra was to be allowed visitation on suitable and proper occasions. Permission to do so was expressly given and granted to Ezra.[317]

Ezra moves on with his life, relocates to New Orleans, and

---

316 1895 Shelby County, Tennessee Marriage Records and 1900 Tennessee Census Records.

317 Memphis, Tennessee Divorce Court Records, July 29, 1901.

marries again within two years to a thirty-three year old Lucille Mallard. He was involved in the manufacturing refining business, but he is eventually the president of a lard manufacturing company. He lived in a $10,000 home with a servant and chauffer but died in 1938.[318] When William, known as Willie, registers for the draft in 1917, he was attending A&M College later known as Mississippi State in Starkville.

Jessie was always very close to her brother Alexander Cogle McKissack, who was seven years older. He graduated from Yale University in 1852 as she was planning to graduate from the Columbia Athenaeum girls' school a year later. After graduation, he returned to Spring Hill to study law, but he was uninterested in that area and decided to go to Pulaski about forty miles south where he was involved in cotton and wool manufacturing.[319] His oldest brother James Thomson went to Jackson College and was engaged in the grocery and general merchandise business in Spring Hill. He married Sylvina C. Rowe in 1845 and moved to the Pulaski area nine years later. He became involved in building the old courthouse and a number of business blocks. He also purchased land near Vale Mills and was engaged in farming and manufacturing for twenty-five years.[320]

Alexander met Eliza Jane Aykroyd who was born in New York but was teaching music in Nashville along with her mother and a sister. They had been living in Columbia while Eliza was attending the Columbia Institute along with her sister Maria, and their mother was teaching music and piano. After graduation in 1845, Eliza became part of the Institute faculty teaching music, harp, and guitar. Her sister Maria graduated two years later and joined the faculty teaching music and piano. Rev. Franklin Gillette Smith left the Institute in 1852 after a scandal and established the

---

318 1920 and 1930 New Orleans, Louisiana Census Records.
319 Nathaniel Cheairs Hughes, Jr., *Yale Confederates: A Biographical Dictionary*, (University of Tennessee Press: 2008), p.141.
320 *The Goodspeed History of Giles County of Tennessee,* (Nashville: The Goodspeed Publishing Co. 1887).

Columbia Athenaeum. They must have relocated to the Nashville area about this time since none of them are listed on the faculty of either school.[321] Jessie Peters was acknowledged as playing the harp beautifully, and no doubt knew the family very well. Eliza and Alexander married on August 10, 1854, but within two years,[322] they were moving to Holly Springs, Mississippi to an 800 acre cotton plantation that had been owned by his father. Since there was no will after the death of William McKissack, Alexander bought out his siblings' parts.[323]

Their lives were interrupted by the war, and Alexander enlisted in Company D (Jeff Davis) rifles in Holly Springs. He eventually returned home to raise a squadron of cavalry fighting under General Earl Van Dorn and embarrassing U. S. Grant by raiding Holly Springs and seizing a vast amount of stores. Eliza and some other wives whose husbands were away in the War, spent a great deal of time in Pensacola, Florida, and must have relocated there shortly after the War started. One of the soldiers who had been in the University of Mississippi with Thomas Peters was stationed in Warrington at Camp Davis. He mentions seeing her and several other wives while visiting the area just shortly after the War began.[324]

Alexander spent four years in the war and surrendered with General Nathan B. Forrest at Gainesville, Alabama, on May 12, 1865.[325] He returned home to his Holly Springs plantation, but finances were not what they had been before the war.

Eliza became the founding head of music at the University of North Texas College of Music that was then known as Normal

---

321 Female Institute and Athenaeum Student Records, School Catalogue and Guardian Records, 1850s.

322 Judith Parham Scoville, descendent of Lucy McKissack Parham, personal recollections of family sent to Susan Cheairs' descendent, January 27, 1974, p.2.

323 Hubert H. McAlexander, *Strawberry Plains Audubon Center*, University Press of Mississippi: 2008), p. 50.

324 Jennifer W. Ford, *Op. Cit.*, p. 48.

325 *Op. Cit.*, Hughes.

Conservatory of Music. It was a part of Texas Normal College and Teacher Training Institute that was founded in 1890 as a private institution. Today, the College of Music is a comprehensive school with the largest enrollment of any institution accredited by the National Association of Schools of Music. It is the oldest and the first in the world offering a degree in jazz studies. Since the mid 1900s, the College of Music has been among the largest in the country. Eliza was recommended for the position by Bishop Charles Quintard of Tennessee, U. S. Senator Edward C. Walthall of Grenada, Mississippi, under whom Thomas Peters was studying law at the time of his death, and Orville Brewer of Chicago. She was highly recommended for the college position as pianist and vocalist having studied in Boston and New York. She remained at the college for two years and then went to the New England Conservatory to study music during 1895-1896. The College faced a difficult economy during the first three years and did not have one faculty member from the original group by the end of that time. Eliza was listing her permanent address as Oxford, Mississippi. A codicil to her will was signed by Mrs. James Gowen Sheegog who lived in Rowan Oak located in Oxford that was built by her father-in-law. In later years, this would be the home of William Faulkner.[326]

While visiting Jessie in Memphis in September of 1898, Alexander died at her home from a heart condition. He was buried the next day in Jessie's family plot in Elmwood Cemetery next to Dr. Peters with one plot left between them. Jessie held a mortgage on her brother's plantation, but his wife turned the management of the land over to George Finley. Eliza died about sixteen months later and left the plantation in Holly Springs to her sister's bachelor son since she and Alexander had only one daughter who died early in life. The nephew died nine years later without a will, and the land passed further from the McKissack family.[327] Eliza was buried

---

326 "Eliza Jane McKissack," Wikipedia, The Free Encyclopedia, December 5, 2010.
327 *Op. Cit.*, McAlexander.

in Mt. Olivet Cemetery in Nashville with other Aykroyd family members.

After graduating from Cumberland University, George, Jr., returned to Memphis and was elected in November 1874 to the lower house of the General Assembly. By the time he was 25, he was elected to the State Legislature and again two years later serving on the Judiciary and Finance Committees. Within a year later, he declined the nomination of the Democratic convention to the State Senate but was elected attorney general of Shelby County that he held eight years. In 1875 he formed a law partnership with Luke W. Finney that lasted for nine years in the firm of Finlay & Peters. He was known as a skillful pleader but had perfected himself in common law. Although he was later to be known as a skillful criminal lawyer, he was not known in this area until after 1883.[328]

Although George was a lawyer and a practioner in every sense of the word, and he rarely took any part in political contests, he was always active in municipal affairs. He succeeded in 1879 in conducting the negotiations between the committee of creditors and the citizens to a successful termination. He was quiet in demeanor but argumentative in the conduct of a lawsuit. He was always courteous and especially to those who were younger in the profession, kind, even tempered, and made friends everywhere he went.[329]

On June 13, 1872, George married Katie B. Greenlaw of Memphis. In an unusual twist of outcome, the daughter of Martin Cheairs in whose home George senior had killed General Earl Van Dorn, was married to a member of the Greenlaw family.[330]

A month after Christmas in 1892 in Memphis on an icy day in mid afternoon, nineteen year old Alice Mitchell stopped to pick up her neighbor and twelve year old nephew for an afternoon outing.

---

328 "Conscious to the End," *The Commercial Appeal,* Sunday Morning, December 9, 1906, p. 1.
329 *Ibid.*
330 Shelby and Maury Counties, Tennessee Marriage Records.

Alice and her friend Frederica Ward had attended Miss Higbee's School, one of the finer schools in Memphis at the time. Alice had given Freda a ring and planned to dress as a man so that they could get married possibly in St. Louis. When Freda became interested in a man and returned the ring to Alice, she was devastated. She drove her buggy down the cobblestones leading down to the public steamboat landing near the train station knowing that Freda was leaving. She first drove to the home where Freda and her sister were staying and followed them as they went to the steamboat that would take them home to Gold Dust, Tennessee, just fifty miles north. Alice had taken her father's razor and when she saw her chance, she slashed seventeen year old Freda Ward's throat and left her dying on the railroad tracks.[331]

Alice ran back up the incline to reach her buggy and drove home. She was quoted as telling her mother, "I loved her so I couldn't help it."[332] Her neighbor was arrested as an accessory and was represented by Malcolm Patterson, who also lived in the neighborhood. He would later be elected to Congress and governor fifteen years later.[333]

Attorney General George Peters was the highly successful prosecuting attorney in a case that would be the beginning of much controversy. It was the first time that the word "lesbian" was actually used to identify the homosexuality of a woman.[334] The legal protectors for the defense represented the most influential in Memphis. Pat Winters was a constitutional lawyer known as "one of the shrewdest attorneys in Memphis" who gave assistance in research. George was no stranger to sexual misbehaver, insanity, and murder as he had to deal with his father murdering a Confederate general, a stepmother's infidelity, and the suicide of his brother Thomas. He was assisted in the prosecution by a multitude of very

---

331 Lisa Duggan, *Sapphic Slashers: Sex, Violence, and American Modernity*, (Duke University Press: 2000), p. 9-10.
332 *Ibid.*, p.10-11.
333 *Ibid,*, p. 74.
334 *Ibid.*, p. 28.

young assistants who were facing quite a challenge. Both sides had to present their case before Judge Julius DuBoise, who was unconventional, feared, and detested. Son of a wealthy planter, he was a Confederate soldier, early leader in the Tennessee Ku Klux Klan, and editor of the *Memphis Public Ledger*.[335]

Alice's father was the retired senior partner of furniture makers Mitchell and Bryson. He accompanied his daughter to jail and hired the best lawyers. Freda's father was a former machinist with the Memphis Fertilizing Company as well as a merchant and planter in Gold Dust.[336] Both families were affluent and expected the best from their daughters since they attended Miss Higbee's School for Young Ladies. The school had been the location for some 300 girls to be educated in being submissive Christian wives and mothers.[337]

After each side presented all the evidence, the jury was out for only twenty minutes and then declared that Alice to be insane and to be sent to the Western State Insane Asylum at Bolivar on August 1.[338] Newspapers reported that she died in 1898 from consumption since she had been "wasting away" for some time before her death. On the other hand, she had actually improved and appeared at two dances just days before her death. In an interview several years later, those close to the case said that she actually jumped into a water tank on top of the building and drowned.[339]

At the close of his term as prosecuting attorney, the year of his most famous case, and serving eight years as attorney general, George entered the firm of General Luke E. Wright and Major E. E. Wright. General Luke Wright was hired by Alice Mitchell's father as one of the defending attorneys.[340] He had entered the Confederate Army when he was only fifteen and fought at Stone River, Chickamauga, Franklin, Nashville, and Mobile. After the

---

335 *Ibid.*, p.75.
336 *Ibid.*, p. 53.
337 *Ibid.*, p. 43-44.
338 *Ibid.*, p. 74-75.
339 *Ibid.*, p. 195.
340 Conscious to the End," *Commercial Appeal*, December 9, 1906, p. 1.

war, he entered the University of Mississippi and studied law in his father's office. His eldest son Eldridge, whose mother was Katherine Semmes, a daughter of Admiral Raphael Semmes of the Confederate States Navy, joined the firm after he graduated from the University of Virginia and became one of Tennessee's most leading attorneys. He married George's daughter Minnie.[341] After George served as attorney general, he was elected county attorney of Shelby County that he held for four years. He was always considered able, brief, and concise that made him one of the leading attorneys of the South.[342]

George and Katie had five girls and two boys with only one girl dying as an infant. Katie died in March 1897 at the age of 42.

In the summer of 1906 the doctors diagnosed George with malaria since he was suffering from severe stomach pain and suggested that he should travel to a higher altitude. He went to Colorado Springs, Colorado, and after being there for a month, he began to show improvement. He took a turn for the worst when the pain in his stomach became so intense that it was necessary to administer opiates *(any medicine containing opium)* at times. A doctor from that area was called in on the case, and it was his decision that George was in a serious condition, and an operation was his only chance for recovery. Because of his advanced age, it would be a most delicate procedure. George agreed after realizing how serious he was and gave his consent. Although the surgery was successful for nine days, complications and kidney failure caused his deterioration, and he died seventeen days after his surgery. His death certificate indicated that he died on December 8, would have been 57 a month later, and his death was due to abscess of the liver. His daughter Evelyn and son Arthur accompanied their father's body on the Rock Island Railroad that arrived in Memphis the next

---

341 John Trotwood Moore and Austin P. Foster, *Tennessee, The Volunteer State, 1769-1923*, Vol. 2, (Illinois: S. J. Clarke Publishing Co.,1923).
342 *Op. Cit.*, Conscious.

day. The body was taken to his home where the funeral was held, and he was buried in Elmwood Cemetery.[343]

The city of Memphis took Jessie to court in 1909 because she refused to give a right of way. The city was opening, widening, extending, and improving Rayner Street for a street purpose. It was necessary for the city to acquire certain real estate along that street. The sheriff went to her house to notify Jessie that she was petitioned to appear in court on Saturday, February 20, at 10:00 in the morning. A Cost Bond in the sum of $250 was placed against her, but the case was dismissed when she settled on the 10th.[344]

Jessie was concerned about what became the Great War and later known as World War I that began in 1914. Her grandsons would be the age to have to serve in the military. She wrote a letter to her niece who was the daughter of her sister Lucy. It does not have a date, but she states that she is four miles from the river and in the city limits. It refers to her property in Arkansas, the flowers in bloom, but it being cold and sleeting that happens quite often in spring around Easter. The reference to Lusie may be Medora's daughter Lucy who was born in 1902 and needed extra care because of her epilepsy:

> Are you much concerned about the war? I live four miles from Miss. River yet I am in city limits.
> Memphis is a big town four miles wide & I don't know how long. I tell you they both in a lot of cotton patches and cornfields. People are always writing to me to buy my home here & my plantation in Ark & even my wild lands in Lawrence. I say what I have is better than anybody else. I tell them yes I'll sell one hundred thousand for my home & as much for my plantation.
> After three weeks of warm summer time & all the flowers in bloom—this morning it is cold & sleeting. I believe the war scare has subsided & there'll be no fight=My opinion is that Spain thinks England will assist us & she knows we can whip her off the face of the earth & England can sweep her from the sea. Kind regards to your husband & love to Lucy

---

343 *Ibid.*
344 Memphis, Tennessee Circuit Court Records, February 1909.

& yourself. Lusie sends love Write & tell me something about yourself.

Affectionately
Aunt Jessie

My Residence

Robert Edward Lee Peters known as "Pete" lived with Jessie until he married nineteen year old Emma Clark in 1902. She was from Water Valley in Yalobusha County, Mississippi, where her father was a carpenter. Since Dr. Peters left him land, he and his wife went to live near Marianna, Arkansas, on the land that was referred to as "Mound Place" in Lee County. They had two daughters named Emma Lee and Virginia Clark. Pete was known as a prominent planter, and his splendid home on the plantation at Gassett was considered an open house. They were always surrounded by their friends and were entertaining regularly.[345] Although he was 42, he had to register for the draft in 1918. The description of him was of medium height and build with gray eyes and black hair.

Medora's oldest son Francis left for the Panama Canal Zone sometime after 1910. He was an operator in the Pacific lock and worked there for many years. The first time that he came home to Memphis was seven years later through southern ports to New Orleans. His New Jersey born wife Josephine was with him. She operated a telegraph in the same area of Balboa, Panama that they called home.[346]

On November 30, 1917, Clara Polk Peters known for almost fifty years as Sister Mary Paula died in St. Louis, Missouri, at 4:30 am. Her voice had failed prematurely because it was literally worn out from singing. She gave no regretful thoughts to what might have been, but instead turned her energies into other forms of usefulness. At the age of 65, she had to have one of her eyes removed. Although it was a constant form of irritation and inconvenience in her work, she never expressed regret or impatience. Instead, on the anniversary of the operation, she offered the other eye to God. She said that they both were His and He

---

345 "Death Claims R. E. L. Peters," *Marianna Courier*, April 21, 1928.
346 Panama Canal Zone 1930 Census.

might do with them as He pleased. She told one of the Sisters, "If God wishes me to grope my way through life, His holy Will be done."[347]

She was becoming very frail although no one thought that she was in a dying condition. She was preparing for the Renewal of Vows, and though she was not well, bronchial pneumonia developed. For nine days she lingered and was given Holy Communion every day after the anointing. When she realized that there was no hope, she spoke lovingly to ever one and appreciated every kindness. Perfectly resigned, gentle and patient, her suffering was long but without struggle. Conscious most of the time, she was surrounded by the Mother Superior and Sisters who were praying for her with heavy hearts. She was 69, and if she had lived one more year, she would have celebrated her golden jubilee in the convent. Many outside the cloister mourned her death because of the wide connections that she had with the public.[348]

She had lost all three of her brothers, but her obituary listed only the late George Peters, a prominent attorney of Memphis, and her niece, Miss Minnie Peters who married Gen. Luke Wright. She had three other nieces and two nephews. No mention was made of Jessie, who would live four more years after Clara's death, her half brother and sisters or their children. The funeral of Sister Mary Paula Peters was held in the convent chapel at 8:30 am the next day with Rev. J. J. McGlynn officiating and Rev. J. J. O'Brien reading the mass and was buried in Calvary Cemetery.[349]

A former student wrote a letter to the convent about the loss of Sister Mary Paula:

> My dear Mother   December 12, 1917
> Though late in telling you of my deep sympathy for the great loss the community have sustained in the death of dear Sister Mary Paula, my indeared, I should say <u>our</u> prayer ways of the cross and communicant have been generously offered

---

347 Sisters of the Visitation, B. V. M., From our Monastery of St. Louis, Missouri, November 30, 1917.
348 *Ibid.*
349 "Sister Mary Peters, Academy of Visitation Teacher of Music, Dies," *St. Louis Globe-Democrat,* ,December 1, 1917.

for this dear soul, for the community wholly supernatural, made her an object of reverent admiration to the youth of that day. All seemed to come under her influence. The giddy as well as the serious-minded, the quick-witted and the dullards all alike found her ever calm, gentle, self-poised and extremely kind because she drew her sweetness from the Heart of her spouse whom she loves so well and served so faithfully. Maryville individually and collectively inquired daily of her during her brief illness.

Dear Sister Mary Paula seemed to be such a part of the dear La Cass Avenue house, that it seems hard for the generations of that time to consider her away from it. Her Charming personality and a certain aloofness that I know now have been an atmosphere we confidently wish that her days of waiting may be shortened and that her visions may be hers and that in the sweet rapidness of eternal love she will remember those still struggling here below.

With affectionate remembrances to all the dear sisters whom I know and whom I do not know. I am dear Mother, a grateful old pupil

Mary Reid

All of Medora's thirteen living children were now grown and making lives for themselves. Henry Joyner joined the United States Marine Corps on June 5, 1918. His twin brother Columbus Bierce called "Coll" was in Panama until he enlisted in the Tennessee National Guard the year before Henry. The next year he received a lieutenant's commission and served with the 30th Division in the Somme and Ypres-Lys offensives and the breaking of the Hindenburg Line.[350]

Kate Tomson went to see Francis in Panama in August 1910[351] and visited a second time before she was able to get a job on June 19, 1916. She was hired as a clerk in accounting at a salary of $50 per month. Her health examination indicated that she was almost 5'6" and weighed 110 pounds, her eyesight was 20/40 and 20/20, but she still wore glasses, and she had appendicitis within the last five

---

350 "Col. Lenow to End Army Service," *The Commercial Appeal,* July 23, 1951.

351 "Cedric," Ship records, August 1910.

years that lasted 25 days. Instead of listing Francis as next of kin, she listed Columbus Bierce as the brother to contact in the area in case of an emergency. She is such a good employee that by October her salary is increased to $60 per month.[352]

By the next year, she had accumulated 28 days and asked for a leave of absence. She had been occupying bachelor quarters at House 343, Ancon, Canal Zone but wanted to be paid in cash at the pay office in Balboa Heights. Employees who took their leave in the United States were to apply to the The Chief of Office, The Panama Canal, Washington, D. C., for return transportation and sailing instructions immediately after landing, forwarding the order with their application. If they delayed, they may not get accommodations. They were to pay immediately and the ticket would be held at the office until noon of the sailing day and then taken to the dock. The employee was expected to report for duty promptly at the end of their leave. They could be given seven days for a long distance if beyond their control.[353] Kate's leave began on June 8, but she resigned when she returned to take effect July 5. Her workmanship and conduct had been excellent, but she did not list why she was resigning.[354]

Kate was going to marry the brown haired, brown eyed and tall George Myers Guerin from St. Louis.[355] His father was a well known photographer and made a very good living photographing well-to-do citizens in the area. Between sittings, he would heap hours on more ambitious undertakings such as crowded sentimental scenes usually built around the doings of children as well as what then passed for bachelor art.[356]

---

352 U. S. National Archives and Records Administration, Panama Employment records, Isthmian Canal Commission and The Panama Canal Information Ship, June 16, 1916.
353 *Ibid.*, The Panama Canal Request for Leave of Absence in Excess of Five Days.
354 *Ibid.* The Panama Canal Executive Office and Termination of Service Blank for Employees on the Gold Roll.
355 WWI Draft Registration Card, September 22, 1918.
356 "F. W. Guerin," *American Heritage*, Vol. 3, No. 3, 1982, pp. 65-73.

Arundel was an old family name by someone who invented a very elaborate buggy that aristocracy of the time was very fond. Arundel was a town in England, and the family descended from the Earl and named several of their children by this name.[357] Arundel Lenow served in France during WWI. When he returned, he worked for the newspaper in Memphis.[358]

By January 3, 1921, Jessie called "Grand" by her family turned 83. She had been living in her house located in Memphis for 42 years. She would often tell her granddaughters, "I wouldn't marry anyone who didn't have as much money as I do. I'm not going to sleep with any man and call him Mr." It was the custom that wives always refer to their husband as Mr. especially in public.[359] Jessie died on July 16 of cholera morbus. It is a noninfectious rarely fatal cholera with diarrhea and cramps. It is usually caused by contaminated foods. The inflammation was caused most often by bacteria or other toxins, parasites or adverse reaction to something in the diet or medication. The most serious complication was dehydration.

Jessie had offered her home as a site for a park, but when she died, they stated in her obituary that the offer was not yet accepted. She was buried on July 18 next to Dr. Peters in Elmwood Cemetery.[360] Her will was filed two days after her funeral:

LAST WILL AND TESTAMENT OF MRS. JESSIE H. PETERS

FILED JULY 20TH, 1921

I, Mrs. Jessie H. Peters, of Memphis, Tenn., being of sound and disposing mind and memory, hereby make, publish and declare this my last will and testament, revoking all other wills heretofore made by me.

---

357 "Oh, the 'Agony' of it all," *The Amazing Kate*. History, genealogy/Gather, May 22, 2008.

358 "Arundel Lenow," *The Commercial Appeal*, January 3, 1970.

359 Interview with Laura W. Walker, Granddaughter of Medora Peters Lenow, Memphis, Tennessee, August 2009.

360 *The Commercial Appeal*, Memphis, Tennessee, July 18, 1921.

I.

I desire all my just and legal debts paid as soon as practicable after my death.

II.

I devise and bequeath my entire property, real, personal and mixed, and wherever situated, to the Memphis Trust Company, in trust as follows:

The said Memphis Trust company shall take and hold possession and control of all my estate, collect all the rents, income and profits of my said estate, pay all taxes, costs and charges incident to the administration of the trust, and divide the net proceeds equally between my daughter, Kate Chalmers Peters, my daughter Medora Wharton Lenow, and my son Robert Edward Lee Peters, for and during the term of their natural lives and at the death of either of my said children the share of the deceased parent shall be paid to such child or children as he or she may leave until such child or children as he or she may leave until such child or children reaches the age of twenty one years, when this trust shall cease and determine as to said child.

Should either one of my said children die leaving more than one child surviving, then the said trustee shall settle with each of said children surviving as he or she arrives at the age of twenty one years.

Should either of my children die, leaving no child or children surviving them, then the share of the income of the child so dying shall go the surviving son or daughter as the case may be, to be held by the Memphis Trust Company in trust for such survivor for life and that the termination of the life estate for his or her children as hereinbefore set forth.

The share of any devisee or legatee under this will who may be a female shall be to her sole, separate and exclusive use, free from the debts, contracts, obligations, or marital rights of any husband they may ever have.

III.

I appoint the Memphis Trust Company guardian of such descendants of my children as may be minors at the death of their parents, as well as testamentary trustee. During the continuation of this trust, the said Memphis Trust company is authorized and empowered to make such changes in the investment of the trust property as to it may seem advisable, and for such purpose it is authorized to make such sales of any portion of my estate, and the deed of my said Executor shall vest a good title in the purchaser, the purchaser in all cases being relieved of the duty of looking to the application of the proceeds of any sale.

IV.

The Memphis Trust Company is hereby appointed executor of this will in each of the States in which my property is situated.

I desire the Memphis Trust Company to employ my son, Robert Edward Lee Peters, to manage my plantation in Arkansas so long as said property may belong to my estate at a salary reasonable and commensurate with the services rendered.

In witness thereof, I have hereunto set my hand, this the 9th, day of October, 1902. Interlineations & erasures made before signing.

Mrs. Jessie H. Peters.

We, the undersigned, do hereby certify that Mrs. H. Peters signed the foregoing instrument of writing in our presence, and declared the same to be her last Will and Testament, and we, as subscribing witnesses, in the presence of the testator, and in the presence of each other, have hereunto set our hands at her request.

W. A. Steward
W. H. Singelton
Jno. H. Watkins

CODICIL

I hereby modify the fourth clause of the above will executed Oct. 9, 1902 as follows:

I desire the Memphis Trust Company to employ my son, Robert Edward Lee Peters, to manage my plantation in Arkansas as so long as said property may belong to my estate, but he is to receive no salary for such services, except that he may live on the plantation while acting as such manager.

In all other respects, my said will of October 9th, 1902 is hereby republished and confirmed.

Mrs. Jessie H. Peters

Jessie Helen McKissack Peters (1838-1921) Photo courtesy Rippavilla Plantation, Spring Hill, TN.

Left to right: Jessie Peters, Medora Peters Lenow, Kate Peters Holden, Robert Edward Lee Peters

George M. Guerin married to Kate Tomson Lenow, Medora's daughter. They lived and died in Panama Canal Zone. Helene Lenow, Medora's oldest daughter, went to Panama to take care of their three children and married George. Ten days later, he died of appendicitis. Courtesy ancestry.com, passport applications and American deaths in foreign countries.

George B. Peters, Jr., lawyer and attorney general in Memphis, was eight years old when his father and Jessie married. Photo courtesy Commercial Appeal, Dec. 9, 1906.

Alexander Cogle McKissack, Jessie's brother and Yale graduate, who died during a visit at her house. Photo in possession of Manuscripts and Archives, Yale University Library.

Medora's Last Years and Her Family

Medora and Henry's daughter Kate continued to live in Panama where her husband was manager of Angelo-American SS Agencies in Cristabal, Canal Zone. They had two sons and on October 12, 1921, they had a daughter they named Katherine. Twelve days later, Kate died.[361]

By this time, George was manager of Goethals, Wilford & Boyd, Inc. George W. Goethals was appointed by President Roosevelt as Chairman and Chief Engineer of the Isthmian Canal Commission. He served in that position until completion of the Canal construction in 1914 followed by serving as Governor until his resignation three years later.[362]

George was having a difficult time handling three children who were all under the age of five. He contacted Kate's oldest sister Helene to come to Panama and assist in caring for the children. She arrived in March to find the baby in a pitiful physical state, and she immediately began to bring her back to good physical health. George became very ill not long after and asked Helene on his death bed for her to take care of his children and have custody and

---

361 U. S. National Archives and Records Administration, Report of Birth of Children Born to American Parents, American Consular Service, Calon, Panama, July 13, 1922.

362 Panama Canal History, George Washington Goethals Biography, November 6, 2008.

control of them. They got a marriage license on September 25, and George died ten days later on October 5. Three days later, Helene and the children were leaving Cristabal, Canal Zone on a ship to San Francisco.[363]

Helene also had a difficult time when she returned to Memphis maintaining all three children. She eventually allowed George's brother who lived in California to adopt William, the youngest son. Medora tried to help by keeping the children during the day and sometimes for extended periods of time when Helene was trying to work.[364] Henry was not well and died on July 23, 1925, at the age of 69 from pulmonary edema. Medora would follow on October 26, 1931, suffering from arteriosclerosis that is hardening of the arteries with hypertension. She also had a hemorrhage and infected kidneys.[365] The doctor had told her several years before that she had the body of a woman the age of 100 after having so many children.[366]

Francis, the second child of Medora and Henry, was home from Panama to attend the funeral of his mother. He immediately started court proceedings against Helene to adopt Kate's daughter Katherine. He got his brother Henry to be a part of the Petition for Writ of Habeas Corpus and had it filed less than six weeks after Medora's death on December 5 at 10 am. Henry was listed as a citizen of Shelby County, Tennessee, for many years while Francis was a temporary resident of the Canal Zone. They stated that the child was about eleven months of age when her father died, and fourteen to seventeen days previous to the death that George Guerin and Helene Lenow were married. Katherine was born in Panama as well as her two older brothers. While moving to Memphis, Helene allowed a brother of George Guerin to adopt the younger son. They pointed out that Helene had lived at various places since being

---

363 State of Tennessee, Henry J. Lenow and Francis J. Lenow vs. Helene Lenow Guerin, Court testimony, December 22, 1931. p. 1.
364 *Ibid.*
365 Death Certificates for Henry and Medora Lenow.
366 *Op. Cit., Interview Laura W. Walker.*

in Memphis and one time in Hernando, Mississippi. They were contended that most of the time that Katherine had been in the care and custody of Medora. Since the death of their mother Medora Lenow, Helene had the custody and control of Katherine.[367]

Henry claimed that he had practically supported the child most of her life, and actually Helene was in a way dependent on him for support. Henry had given notice to Helene that he was going to give up the house that he had been occupying on January 1. Because Helene was attempting to earn a livelihood by operating a sandwich shop in the basement of the Porter Building, she did not have the time to give the child proper care and supervision or look after her welfare. He stated that she had not done so for the past several years and had left everything for the deceased grandmother and her sister Kate Holden to do in caring for the children.[368]

Francis and Henry claimed that Katherine was illegally restrained of her liberty. They further stated that the present custodian was not her legal guardian and had no legal right any more than they did as relatives, and the best interest of the child was the paramount and control factor in the entire matter. They asserted that the best interest would be promoted by taking the child from its stepmother and placing her in the care and custody of her uncle Francis J. Lenow.[369]

They declared that Helene had sent her sister out to place Katherine in an orphanage and within the previous two years had contemplated such a procedure. They further declared that Helene had said that morning that she had sent Katherine to California the day of the petition in an attempt to evade a hearing in court. She knew that they were going to have a sworn petition before a judge of the Probate Court alleging that Katherine did not have proper or sufficient guardianship. Helene was not mentally, morally or

---

367 Circuit Court of Shelby County, State of Tennessee, Ex Rel Henry J. Lenow and Francis J. Lenow, Petitioner vs. Helene Lenow Guerin, Defendant, No. 31390, December 5, 1931.
368 *Ibid.*, p.2.
369 *Ibid.* ,p. 2-3.

physically able to care for her, and on the advice of their attorney, the warrant was dismissed the day before at noon without any hearing whatsoever. They had maintained that Katherine was a delinquent.[370]

Francis further argued that he earned a substantial salary, had other property and means, and able to properly support, care for, maintain, educate, and rear Katherine. He had brothers and sisters in Memphis and Mississippi who wanted Katherine placed in his custody. He had the desire to adopt her, he was married, and his wife was anxious for him to adopt Katherine since they had no children of their own. He claimed his position was reasonably permanent as he had been employed by the United States Government for twenty-one years. He could retire in eleven or more years with $130 retirement pay. He claimed that living conditions in the Canal Zone were equal to or better than in Memphis. No vagrants existed, no saloons, and no one was allowed in the Canal Zone who was not regularly employed except tourist passing through. Schools were equal to if not better than those in the United States. Health conditions were equally as good; therefore, Katherine's best interest would be promoted by permitting him to adopt her.[371]

The writ of habeas corpus was a command for Helene to bring Katherine before the court. A full and complete hearing was to be made upon the merits. Francis wanted the court to award the custody and control of Katherine to him and that he be permitted to legally adopt her.[372]

Two days later Helene gave an answer to the petition acknowledging the residency of Henry and Francis, she was their sister, stepmother and aunt of Katherine now ten years old. She did allow the youngest son to be adopted by his father's brother. Helene had the care, custody, and control of both children without any assistance whatsoever because the father left no estate. Although she admitted that she had lived in various places, the children were

---

370 *Ibid.*, p.3.
371 *Ibid.*, p. 3-4.
372 *Ibid.*, p. 4.

not in the care and custody of Medora, other than for eighteen months, Helene and the children lived with her because she was ill and needed attention. Helene was giving attention to her mother and did so up until the time of her death the past October.[373]

As far as her brother Henry supporting Katherine most of her life, he had given nothing. He was living in the house with their mother when Helene was there for the eighteen months taking care of all of them. She did the cooking, house work, and purchased part of the groceries used. Medora was drawing about $180 a month, and Helene declared that Henry got most of it. Any other expenses were paid by their mother, and immediately at her death, Henry informed Helene to find another place to live because he was making other arrangements. She asserted that he was afraid she would ask for assistance and wanted to support the taking of the children from her. She was concerned that no one was considering what would happen to the oldest child. The two children were devoted to each other and to her and separating them would be most cruel to all concerned.[374]

She intended to show the court that she had a good living until the previous two years, but had been financially embarrassed and struggling. This did not prevent her love and devotion to the children or their devotion to her paid her for her efforts in their behalf. She did admit that two years previous that she wrote to Francis asking for assistance from which she received no reply. Since he arrived in Memphis for their mother's funeral, she asked him to buy Katherine a pair of shoes, and he refused. She claimed that Francis was not a fit and proper person to have custody of any child because he did not and never had liked children. His wife would not have time to care for a child because she ran a beauty shop in Panama.[375]

Helene denied that she illegally restrained Katherine of her liberty and had no legal right to the children. She was stepmother and aunt because their father gave Katherine to her at his death. For

---

373 *Ibid.*, Answer of Respondent, December 8, 1931.
374 *Ibid.*, p. 1-2.
375 *Ibid.*, p. 3.

almost ten years, she had reared, educated, and supported Katherine for whom Francis had given nothing. Since the child left Panama, he had not seen her until recently. He had not sent her a Christmas present, nor contributed anything when asked, or had any interest in her. She asserted that although he was related that his character did not constitute the best interest and welfare of Katherine.[376]

As far as placing the children in an orphanage, Helene was offered the position to run the tea room in the Mansfield Arms Apartments. She was not allowed to have the children with her but was forced to take the position. She asked her youngest sister Flora to help temporarily with Katherine until finances improved. She indicated that her sister offered, and for a period of five to six months took care of Katherine until other arrangements could be made. She was not aware that her sister went to an orphanage to place the child as Francis had stated.[377]

Helene questioned the earnings of Francis since his wife was operating a beauty shop in Panama and must not think his salary is enough to support her. She presumed that his wife's shop must be the other property referred to by him. As to the wishes of her brothers and sisters in the matter, they have no voice in the matter since they have done nothing for the children in their lifetime while she maintained, educated, and supported them to the best of her ability and gave them the love of a mother. She also did not believe that the living conditions were better or vagrants and saloon reputation were as stated, but he must know about saloons. She had heard Francis state that a cut on his face was received during a fit in a saloon in Panama. The class of society that Francis moves was not known; however, when Helene asked about her old friends there and those of her late husband, he responded, "High hatted him and knew nothing of them." Those she had mentioned were of the best society and unquestionably he did not get to the best society. With all that was stated, Helene could see no reason why it would be for the best interests of Katherine to place her

---

376 *Ibid.*
377 *Ibid.*, p. 4.

in the hands of someone who was practically a stranger and whose living conditions could not be determined. After Helene answered the petition, she asked that it be dismissed.[378]

On the cloudy and rainy day of December 22, Helene had two brothers and two sisters testify against her in court. The local papers said that the little girl herself said that she wanted to stay with her big brother who was now 13 and her stepmother and aunt who is the only mother she had ever known.[379]

Henry gave evidence that as an operator of a tea shop, she had reached the peak of her earning power in her profession and could not adequately support the two children. Under direct examination by Luther H. Graves, he stated, "I think it is to the best interest of Katherine that she go with my brother. My sister doesn't seem to love Katherine, and she is always taking George's part. She whips little Katherine when she should whip George. George was allowed to run wild, that he played hookey constantly, and roamed the streets until a late hour. Once I picked him up down on the river front while I was getting ready to go hunting."

Lila L. Willins told the court, "Little Katherine needs love, affection, and clothing. My sister never seems to manifest any devotion for the child, and she lets George fight on the streets."

Flora Martin, the youngest of the sisters who kept Katherine, gave evidence, "Sister never seems to have any love for Katherine. I don't believe she loves her. I think that Francis should be allowed to take her."

"The Panama Canal Zone is the wealthiest place in the world," claimed Francis in presenting his side. "I am employed in the ship yards there and earn from $285 to $350 a month. I have no children, and I would certainly do all I could for Katherine." This would be four to five thousand dollars by today's standards.

Helene's attorney got Francis to admit in court that that it was the first time that he had seen the child since she was an infant in

---

378 *Ibid.*, p. 4-5.
379 "Drama in Court Centers on Child," *The Commercial Appeal*, Vol. CXXI-No. 176, Tuesday morning, December 22, 1931, p. 1.

Panama. He was in Memphis because of the death of his mother on October 26.

When Helene took the stand, she burst into tears when she proclaimed, "Oh, of course, I love little Katherine." She continued to tell the court of her efforts to earn enough to take care of the children, and said that every member of her family owed her money. She indicated that it was the reason of the supposed ill feeling.

The audience grew in the courtroom among them Judge Capell and Judge Laughlin who had six children and testified to Helene's good reputation. Judge Laughlin, who had known Helene and the whole Lenow family for years, claimed," So far as I know, Mrs. Guerin was an excellent mother and a splendid lady."

In the corridor outside, Katherine and George were sitting with Helene playing and kicking each other under the table. Katherine said that she didn't want to go to Panama but did not testify. "Who would want to go to Panama?" she asked, doing a tap dance. "I'd want to stay with Mama and George."

After the death of their mother Medora, it was revealed that the brothers and sisters got together and all declared that Helene did not seem to love little Katherine and lavished her affections on George. They thought that it was for Katherine's best interest to return to Panama with her Uncle Francis who worked in the ship yards there at a handsome salary. Counter and counter charges flew thick and fast through the court testimony.[380]

In his conclusion about the case, Judge Pittman stated, "There is no doubt but what there is some unkind feeling between Mrs. Guerin and the Lenows. What it is, what is at the bottom of it, I don't know, but in any large family there are certain to be quarrels of some sort—soon forgotten usually. But be that as it may about Panama, I have no doubt that it is a desirable town. Immediate members of my own family have been connected with it for 20 years, so I don't attach much importance to any charges about it not being a healthful place."[381]

---

[380] *Ibid.*

[381] "Court Refuses to Break Up Family," *The Commercial Appeal*, Vol. CXXI-No. 177, Tuesday morning, December 23, 1931, p. 1.

Judge Pittman continued in his philosophic attitude, "I don't understand it to be the right or the duty of a judge to take a child away from one party and give it to another party purely and simply on a financial basis. If that were so, then Rockefeller could come down here and take all of Judge Laughlin's children away from him. The testimony shows that Mrs. Guerin has had a hard struggle, and I know it for a fact that the punishment or lack of punishment of one child or the other never meets with the approval of the whole family clan, but there is not a word against the character of Mrs. Guerin, and it seems to me unthinkable to take away from her the custody of this child."

On the afternoon of December 22, just three days before Christmas and the day that Frances turned 43, the court declared that ten-year-old Katherine Guerin would remain with her stepmother and maternal aunt. The court would thus allow Katherine and her brother George, who was 13, would not be separated. It also meant that her young life would not take up where it began in the Panama Canal Zone where her mother died 12 days after Katherine was born and then her father died about a year later. Judge Pittman concluded, "I have not reached this conclusion through any lack of faith in the character of Mr. Lenow, but the court believes that there is in life that which is much stronger than worldly possessions."

Judge Pittman dismissed the writ for habeas corpus and gave more perspective remarks while outside in the corridor where Katherine danced and skipped. She pinched her brother George and was pinched in return as she was jovial on the decision, "I knew I would not have to go. I love my mamma so and George, too."

The first of January, Henry and Francis Lenow filed a Motion for New Trial in the Circuit Court of Shelby County, Tennessee. They claimed that the court made mistakes in dismissing their petition, that they were not entitled to the custody of the child, and that it was in the best interest of the child to remain with its stepmother and aunt. There was no evidence that a new trial was allowed.[382]

---

382 Circuit Court of Shelby county, State of Tennessee, Ex Rel Henry J. Lenow and Francis J. Lenow, Petitioner vs. Helene Lenow Guerin, Defendant, No. 31390, Motion for New Trial, December 5, 1931.

The great depression began in 1929, and many individuals across the nation suffered financially until well into the 1930s. It was very difficult for men to find jobs to support their families but even more complicated for a woman.

One of the places where Helene lived was in the home of seventy-eight year old Thomas Kader Riddick while she was hostess in the tea shop.[383] He was known as the dean of the Memphis bar and known by his peers for putting a judge on the spot. He defended Mayor E. H. Crump when the state removed him from office along with the vice mayor, city judge, and the police inspector for allowing saloons and houses of ill fame to flourish in Memphis in violation of the law. Riddick died five years later after an illness of several months.[384]

Helene operated the Golden Glow Tea Shop on Main Street in Memphis and later the Little Tea Shop on Popular. She had borrowed money from Edmond Willins to open one of the tea shops although her sister Lila had testified against her in the case about the children.[385] On March 6, 1939, Helene was granted a copyright for a work of art. She developed a red stone teapot with a silver spout that was sufficiently different to warrant protection for the design.[386] In later years, Helene had her sister Lucy, who suffered from epilepsy, living with her in an apartment house across from St. Mary's Cathedral, but she lived less than a year after the death of Helene, who died on June 27, 1960, at the age of 73.[387]

Jessie McKissack Peters' estate had never been settled since she had most of her property put in a trust and only income from the estate had been dispensed. Kate Peters Holden was the only child still

---

383 1930 Shelby County, Tennessee, Census.
384 "T. K. Riddick, Dean of Local Bar, Dies," *The Commercial Appeal*, Memphis, Tennessee Wednesday morning, January 29, 1936, p. 1.
385 *Op. Cit.*, Interview Laura W. Walker.
386 *Catalog of Copyright Entries,* Part 4 "Works of Art," Helene Lenow Guerin #1728.
387 "Mrs. Helene Guerin, Longtime Memphian to be Buried Today," *The Commercial Appeal*, June 27, 1960, p. 27.

living in July 1942. Francis as the child of Medora sold his share in the estate to her son "Willie" for $1,000. He had the papers notarized in the Canal Zone and did not appear in court. Real estate was listed as being located in Crittendon County, Arkansas, and Lawrenceburg, Tennessee. The share was equal to 1/39 of the total estate.[388]

Kate Peters Holden had been a diabetic for several years and had coronary heart disease. She died on March 26, 1943, in Methodist Hospital in Memphis and was buried in Elmwood Cemetery next to her brother William.[389]

Although Josephine Carr Lenow, wife of Francis, came back several times from Panama, he did not return for eighteen years. He had been a foreman in an oil plant when he retired and moved to Florida where he died in 1964. Josephine lived on in the same area for three more years.

Henry Lenow's other plans included marrying Ruby S. Stevens on New Year's Eve after the trial. The marriage was plagued by problems from the beginning. He left after six years and as she stated, without any cause on her part, "He packed his grip, saying that 'He did not care to live with her any longer.'" It was not the first time that he had abandoned her. She took him back several times when he promised to earn a living for the family and do better. He had not contributed anything to her support in the last two years and insisted that he would do nothing to this end in the future.

In the 1939 divorce, she asked that her maiden name be restored, that she receive alimony both temporary and permanent, and that he was to pay the costs. She said that she was living in poverty and unable to bear the expense of the divorce. She was still trying to get him in court in July.[390] Henry had been a salesman, but four years before he died, he moved to San Antonio, Texas, where his younger

---

388 Assignment and Agreement, Book 98, Page 52, Court Records filed in Memphis, Tennessee, August 31, 1942.

389 Obituary, *The Commercial Appeal*, Saturday morning, March 27, 1943, p. 11 and Death Certificate #6138

390 Circuit Court Records of Shelby County, Tennessee, No. 39232, February 1939.

brother Arundel lived with his family. He had been employed as a civil service employee at Kelly Air Force Base when he died of a heart attack in 1952 and was buried in the Sam Houston National Cemetery. His funeral included military services since he served in the U.S. Marines during WWI.

Columbus Bierce called "Coll" was an Army colonel when he retired from his military career in July 1951 after 34 years. When he completed his registration card for WWI, he was a bookkeeper for a company in Memphis, but he was also in the National Guard. A year later he received a lieutenant's commission, and served with the 30th Division in the Somme and Ypres-Lys offensives and in the breaking of the Hindenburg Line during WWI. His last assignment was that of Chief of the Receipts and Disbursement division in the office of the Chief of Finance. He entered the Finance Corps in 1933 and opened the first finance office at Hickam Field, Honolulu in 1940. In 1945 he was transferred to Manila where he was Fiscal Director of American Forces, Western Pacific Command. In appreciation of his work in the Philippines, the Philippine government awarded him the Legion of Honor with the grade of commander for "attention to duty which has been far reaching in the economic and social progress and rehabilitation of the Philippines." He married Mary Sue Bolinger of Ft. Smith, Arkansas, about 1916. Living in Alexandria, Virginia, after retirement, he outlived his twin brother Henry by thirteen years.[391]

Arendel was an advertising salesman for the Memphis *Commercial Appeal* shortly after his return from France during WWI. He left Memphis when he decided to go to San Antonio, Texas in the 1920s. He married Margaret Mivelaz whose father was from Switzerland and was a hotel chef in Little Rock, Arkansas. He and his family lived in San Antonio until his death in 1970.

Medora Lenow known as "Betty" or "Aunt Do" was named after her mother and lived most of her life in Macon, Mississippi. She married Cary Weathers Salter who was a doctor, and together

---

[391] "Colonel Lenow to End Army Service," *Commercial Appeal*, July 23, 1951.

they had four children.³⁹² When Medora was 74, she was declared incompetent to handle her own affairs. The Mississippi Bank and Trust of Jackson was appointed conservator to oversee her affairs. Her youngest son was appointed successor conservator. She died at 93 in 1990 in Manhatten Health Care Center in Jackson, Mississippi.³⁹³

Nell married Harold H. Hansen who was from Denmark.

Lucy lived with Medora until her death and then with different family members. She had to take medication that made her skin and face "pop out," and her face to be quite distorted at times. She died in 1961 and is buried close to her father in Elmwood Cemetery. William Holden bought her interest in Jessie's estate for $1,000 in the same manner as he had bought Francis' share.³⁹⁴

William McKissack known as "Billy" was in the Marine Corps and spent a great deal of his military time in the Republic of Haiti.³⁹⁵ He had been a bookkeeper in the bank but later sold wholesale items. He sold his interest in Jessie's estate to William Holden in April 1942 for $10. The transfer was more specific as the land was listed in Crittenden County, Arkansas, known as Cat Island Plantation. The property was sold in Spring Hill in 1873 and land was swapped for Cat Island. Some years later it was stated the only building on the property was an old fishing cabin. Billy never married and died in 1955.³⁹⁶

Flora known as "Po Po" married Van Martin who was a bookkeeper in a bank and later a manager. She had helped Helene when she kept Katherine and the same time had her brother Billy living with her as well as her daughter.³⁹⁷ She had worked for Union Planters National Bank before her retirement and died of heart

---

392 *Op. Cit.*, Interview Laura W. Walker.
393 U.S. Court of Appeals, Fifth Circuit, January 17, 1977, Estate of Salter v. C. I. R. 545F. 2d 494, January 17, 1977.
394 *Op. Cit.*
395 U. S. National Archives, Microfilm Record Group 127, U. S. Marine Corps 1798-1940.
396 Shelby County, Tennessee, Court Records, "Assignment," April 1942.
397 US 1930 Census, Shelby County, Tennessee.

disease in 1994. She was staying with her mother Medora when she died and supplied the information for the death certificate. For some unknown reason, she indicated that she did not know the name of Medora's parents, her grandmother's maiden name, or where they were born. She was fifteen when her grandmother died and no doubt knew who she was; however, their conversations may have not included the information.[398]

Robert Allyn known as "Bobby" had lived in Indiana for a period of time. He was married to Gladys and had a stepdaughter and stepson. He was a painter and died in 1975.[399] Willie Holden bought Bobby's share of Medora's estate as he had several others. He bought Bobby's his share for $10 in 1945.[400]

Robert Edward Lee Peters outlived his mother by seven years dying at 52 at his home after a brief illness of pneumonia. His remains were taken to Memphis where the funeral was held the next afternoon in the funeral home of J. T. Hinton & Son. He was the only child of Jessie's who was not buried in Boliver or Elmwood Cemetery but instead in Forest Hill. He was a Mason as his father and a Shriner. He was described as one of nature's noblemen who could not be happier than when he was surrounded by friends.[401]

Pete, as he was known to his friends, did not have a will. His wife Emma had to go to court to have herself appointed administrator of his estate. Their children were only 11 and 9 and the estimated value of the estate of Pete was about $9,000. When Emma declared that she would complete an inventory, pay all his debts, and execute a bond that was $18,000, she had no idea that his finances would cause her to have to take some of her own money to pay off his debts.[402]

---

398 Obituary, *The Commercial Appeal*, June 16, 1994.
399 Obituary, *The Commercial Appeal*, Friday, January 17, 1975.
400 Shelby County, Tennessee, Court Records Book 97, Page 118, "Assignment," May 4, 1942.
401 "Death Claims R. E. L. Peters," *Marianna Courier*, Marianna, Arkansas, April 23, 1928.
402 Lee County, Arkansas, Probate Court, "Petition of Mrs. Emma C. Peters for Letters of Administration," April 26, 1928.

Four years later, Emma was continuing to manage the estate by filing in court a final settlement and a petition for discharge.

According to the inventory: Debts:

Assets	$11,677.09	Funeral Expenses	$1,400.00
Paid out	10,749.14	Premiums Surety Bond	194.86
Balance	$ 927.95	Attorney Fee, R. I. Moore	75.00
		Total	$1,269.86

She, therefore, paid out more than she received, and the excess was paid out of the personal money of Emma. The petition stated that she had paid out a considerable amount of her own money. There were tenant accounts that were listed as assets in the amount of $2,916 that were never collected; therefore, they were a loss to the estate. They had mules to die and small bills that were owed by Pete not listed in the inventory. As widow, she took over at the inventory price the commissary, farming implements, mules and horses and allowing for them as cash the amount shown in the inventory as filed when they were not worth as much as stated. She did fulfill all the duties as an administratrix in paying all debts although more than she received and asked that the estate be closed.[403] Her attorney, Robert I. Moore of Memphis wrote a letter to the Judge S. L. Kirkpatrick, Marianna, Arkansas, asking for the paying of the premium on the bond to end. He stated that the estate could have been settled some time before, but they did not get to it. He claimed that, "Womanlike, she did not get receipts for all those debts she paid, and her checks have been misplaced, although I told her in writing in the beginning to keep all these things safely for the purpose of the settlement."[404]

On December 20, 1934, just a year and a half after settling Pete's estate, Emma died. The family indicated that she drank herself

---

[403] Lee County, Arkansas, Probate Court, "Final Settlement of Administratrix and Petition for Discharge," July 25, 1932.

[404] Lee County, Arkansas, Probate Court ,Robert I. Moore, Attorney at Law, Memphis, Tennessee, March 28, 1935.

to death. Within a few months after her death, the court reduced the bond from $9,000 to $250 because she had done everything in payment of debts and the statute of limitations stopped all claims against the estate. The only thing that had not been settled was the inheritance tax.[405]

Two months after Pete died, Emma had made a will:

LAST WILL AND TESTAMENT OF EMMA C. PETERS

I, Emma C. Peters, of Gassett, Lee County, Arkansas, widow of Robert E. Lee Peters, do make and declare this my last will and testament, hereby revoking all other wills made by me.

Item I.

I direct my executors to pay all by just debts including funeral expenses.

Item II.

I give, devise and bequeath to my two children, Emma Lee Peters and Virginia Clark Peters, all my estate, both real, personal, wheresoever situated, in equal shares, one half to each, to their sole and deparate use, free from the debts, contracts or control of any husband they may have. Should either one of my said children die leaving no heirs, then her share shall go to the surviving child in the manner as above set out. Should any one of my said children die leaving heirs, then the share of said child shall go to her said heirs. By the word "heirs" wherever used above, is meant their children or the children of their children

I appoint my friends, Joe V. Lontedonico and William K. Love, both of Memphis, Tenn., executors of this my last will and testament, and relieve them of the obligation of making any bond as such executors.

---

[405] Lee County, Arkansas, Probate Court, "Petition for Reduction of Bond," March 28, 1935.

Witness my signature this 27th day of June 1928.

Emma C. Peters

Emma's daughters were living with her sister Janie in Memphis, but she had to file papers that she was their guardian. The girls were now seventeen and fifteen and Janie Clark was their aunt and nearest relative over twenty-one years of age and living in Shelby County, Tennessee.[406] The girls were going to school at St. Mary's that today is considered the oldest private school in Memphis. St. Mary's was officially consecrated as a parish church in 1858 by Right Reverend James Hervey Otey, the first bishop in Tennessee. He went to Memphis from Columbia just six years previously after establishing the Female Institute with Leonidas Polk. In 1873 Bishop Quintad, who was close friends with the Peters and conducted many of their funerals, asked the Sisterhood of St. Mary's to take over the operation of the school for girls.[407]

When not in school, the girls would spend their time with their guardian aunt and her sister Mrs. Lourette Schuman, another aunt who was widowed. She was the suitable person to be guardian, none had been appointed, and the girls wanted her to be guardian. The estate consisted of $5,000 in bonds and securities in a safety deposit box in the State Savings Bank in Memphis and $906.90 in cash in their mother's name, $1425.14 in the Bank of Commerce and Trust Company, and interest of about 700 acres of wild land in Lawrence County, Tennessee that produced no revenue, and 700 acres in Lee County, Arkansas that was under lease for a term of years and $2,000 rent payable in November of each year.[408]

The land in Lawrence County of which they had a one-third interest was unimproved, mountainous, cut-over land in no state

---

406 Lee County, Arkansas, Probate Court, "Petition for Appointment of Administrator with the Will Annexed," No. 2330, January 15, 1935.
407 St. Mary's Episcopal Cathedral, Memphis, Tennessee, Diocese of West Tennessee, Website 2008-2009.
408 Shelby County, Tennessee, Probate Court,"Petition for appointment of Guardian," January 14, 1935.

of cultivation. It was in the hands of the Bank of Commerce and Trust Company as trustee and executor of Jessie Peters, their grandmother, and would not be released from the trustee until the girls became of age. The same bank had an interest in certain funds and securities and would not be released until they became of age, but they would receive the interest to take care of them. When they became twenty-one, the trustee of the bank would then be in control. There was a loan of $14,150 that securities of $16,500 had been put up as collateral with the State Savings Bank of Memphis. The debts of their mother would consume all of her estate, and they would not realize anything from it. The girls signed the petition along with their single aunt.[409]

A month after Emma's death, her sister Janie filed a Guardian's Bond in court with Fidelity and Guaranty Company, a corporation, as surety, for $7,500. As guardian she would pay all court costs, attorney's fees, and other expenses that may be incurred on account of her failure to properly account for all funds coming into her hands, and would especially receive and account for the $5906.90 she would receive from her sister.[410]

Although their mother left a will and appointed two friends from Memphis as executors, they were told that they could not be appointed according to the law because they were not residents of Arkansas, and they were unable to serve; therefore, they renounced the appointment. W. B. Yancey was appointed administrator of her estate upon the request of Emma's daughters who by then were residents of Shelby County. He was a resident of Gassett, Arkansas, had been handling the plantation of Emma's for several years, and it was then under lease at an annual rental. Taxes and upkeep would have to come out of the rental.[411]

W. B. Yancey gave his first and final report as administrator of Emma's estate a year after her death in Probate Court of Lee County,

---

409 *Ibid.*
410 *Ibid.,* "Guardian's Bond."
411 Lee County, Arkansas, Probate Court, "Petition for Appointment of Administrator with the Will Annexed," No. 2330, January 15, 1935.

Arkansas. Everything was located in Memphis other than $110.60 in the bank in Marianna. Robert I. Moore, Attorney claimed that Emma owed him an $81 balance when she died, but he returned the balance of $4.79 that she had given him to pay inheritance tax. Yancey collected all the personal assets, paid all debts including inheritance tax, and the judge closed the estate.[412]

Seven years after their father died, Emma and Virginia filed a Receipt and Waiver of Emma Lee Peters and Virginia Clark Peters in the Probate Court of Lee County, Arkansas. At eighteen and sixteen, they acknowledged that they had received all shares and interests of the estate of their father. Their mother paid all debts and fully administered the estate, all formalities of every kind in connection with the closing, and they requested the estate be closed by the court. They signed the statement, and it was followed by a statement by their guardian Janie Clark. She in turn repeated the same in that her sister had paid all the debts, many out of her own funds, and requested that the state close the estate.[413]

William Robert Holden had dated Virginia for several years. She had been married previously and had two children and was not liked by many members of Willie's family. On the other hand, not many members were fond of Willie and thought that he was pompous and arrogant. He attempted to buy most of the shares of Medora's children and attempted to get the "Big House" in Arkansas. The daughters of Pete Peters inherited the land that their father received in Dr. Peters' will. It continues to remain in the family although the house was destroyed several years ago.[414]

---

412 Lee County, Arkansas, Probate Court, "First and Final Report of W. B. Yancey, Administrator C. T. A. of the Estate of Emma C. Peters, Deceased and Petition for Closing of Estate and Discharge," June 1936.
413 Lee County, Arkansas, Probate Court, "Receipt and Waiver of Emma Lee Peters and Virginia Clark Peters," April 12, 1935.
414 Interview of Rosemary Harper and Butch Harper, grandson of R. E. L. Peters., November 1, 2010.

Emma Clark Peters, wife of Robert Edward Lee Peters. Lived on plantation north of Marianna, AR that continues to be in great grandson of Dr. Peters and Jessie, Butch Harper's family. Photo courtesy of Butch Harper and Rosemary Harper family.

Emma Lee Peters Barrow, daughter of Robert Edward Lee Peters. Photo courtesy of Butch Harper and Rosemary Harper family.

Virginia Clark Peters, daughter of Robert Edward Lee Peters, and her husband Robert Harper. Photo courtesy of Butch Harper and Rosemary Harper family.

Columbus Bierce "Col" Lenow, twin brother of Henry Joiner Lenow, fourth and fifth child of Medora. Photo courtesy "Army Service," Commercial Appeal, Memphis, TN, July 23, 1951.

Helene Lenow Guerin, Medora oldest child who married her sister's husband George Guarin and raised two of their children. Photo courtesy "Mrs. Helene Guerin," Commercial Appeal, Memphis, TN, June 27, 1960.

Lila Lenow Willins, Medora Peters Lenow's third child, was on stage in New York for five years before returning to Memphis, TN. Photo courtesy Laura Willins Walker, daughter of Lila.

Family Tree

McKissack Family

Thomas McKissack (1756-1826) married Lucy Hudson (March 21, 1746-July 25, 1825) in Oct. 1780.

Their children were:

1. William McKissack (November 14, 1781-February 28, 1855) married Rebecca Sallard (abt.1793-1819) in 1814 in North Carolina

    Their child was:

    Eleanor Washington (October 3, 1815-January 15, 1892) married Orville Washington McKissack (November 3, 1809-March 24, 1887) on October 15, 1833, Lawrence County Alabama

    Their children were:

    Alonzo (January 14, 1835-February 19, 1905) married
      Almira Hardeman (May 30, 1845-March 3, 1900)
      September 1, 1880
    Susan R. (1837-)
    Archibald (1841-) married

Lena Belle (1839-1895) married Robert Irwin Moore (1841-1924) April 17, 1865

Orville W., Jr. (January 14, 1845-1915) married Mary Elizabeth McKissack (1855-1935) September 6, 1897

James T. (March 16, 1848-)

Anthula (1845-) never married

Lucy (1848-)

John W. (March 16, 1849-April 5, 1923) married Mary Robena Pope (October 23, 1844-April 10, 1915) January 11, 1877

Bud (1857-

Married Jeannett Susan Buxton Cogle Thomson (November 16, 1803-May 1, 1842) on December 5, 1820 in North Carolina

Their children were:

Susan Peters (July 4, 1821-June 15, 1893) married Nathaniel Francis Cheairs (December 6, 1818-January 2, 1917) September 2, 1841

James Thomson (October 30, 1823-1892) married Sylvania C. Rowe (1822-1880) February 1, 1845 She was from Maine.

Thomas Gorham (November 7, 1825-April 21, 1830)

Don Juan Halensen (January 12, 1828-)

Alexander Cagle (April 30, 1831-October 6, 1898) married Eliza Jane Aykroyd (December 11, 1828-January 5, 1900) August 10, 1854

Lucy Hudson (August 11, 1834-March 16, 1885) married William Pope Parham (February 10, 1830-March 9, 1915) February 6, 1853

Jessie Helen (January 3, 1838-1921) married George Boddie Peters (1814-1889) June 1, 1858

William (April 2, 1842-1843)

Married Arabella White (1805-1855) September 13, 1843/ Divorced about 2 years later

2. Archibald McKissack (January 30, 1789-1869) married Susan Harrison (1790-May 23, 1886) about 1806

Their children were:

>Marcus ( ) married Sarah Grimes (March 4, 1807-)
>Orville Washington (November 3, 1809-March 24, 1887) married Eleanor Washington McKissack (November 3, 1809-March 24, 1887) October 15, 1833
>Meleana Jones (1812-1864) married John F. Lightfoot (1805-1852) 1833
>Thomas J. ( ) married Eliza Jane Marr (1818-) February 15, 1838
>John (1819-)
>James (1821-)
>Martha Louise ( ) married Col. Nathaniel Dandridge ( ) January 6, 1824
>Emily (or Emma) Almira ((1826-) married David C.Pryor (May 30, 1826-) November 2, 1841
>Cynthia Mozelle (August 4, 1827-May 3, 1886) married Dr. Joseph Webb Morris (March 25, 1819-October 4, 1875) November 12, 1855
>Lucy Isabella (March 23, 1827-October 11, 1920) married James Madison
>Armstrong (1824-1855) December 27, 1852 married Greene D. Campbell (1823-1904) April 22, 1861
>Robert Brown (September 4, 1832-1886) married Ellen Adeline Vernon (February 8, 1835-December 14, 1915) 1859 Married Mary Jane Manire (1842-1923)

3. Spivey McKissick (September 18, 1790-June 3, 1864) married Susannah Peter Thomson Jefferies s (1770-1840) April 7, 1813

Their children were:

William Married Musie Barlow } Jessie McKissack Peters indicated in one of her letters this information that cannot be verified.
John

Her child was:

Jeannett Susan Buxton Cogle Thomson (November 16, 1803-May 1, 1842)

Spivey McKissick (September 18, 1790-June 3, 1864) married Eliza B. Smizer (October 13, 1809-August 23, 1872) on October 31, 1842

Their children were:

Mary S. (January 7, 1845-June 26, 1853)
Lucy Ann (November 8, 1846-1921)
Son (June 11, 1845)

4. Susan (1795-1833) married George Simmons (1785-1833) in 1816 Giles County, Tennessee

Their children were:

Sarah (1810-)
Arthur (1811-)
Avis Luvene (March 8, 1808-)
Henritta (1813-)
George Wiles (1825-)
Margaret (1826-)
John (1830)
Artelia (1833-)

5. Rebecca (1782-1826) married Wilson Jones, Jr. (1779-1818) March 26, 1803

Their children were:

Pamela

Susan

Lucinda Williams (1802-1845)

Calvin M. (1810-1868) married Mildred Williamson ( ) October 15, 1835

Thomas McKissack Jones (December 16, 1816-March 13, 1892) married Marietta Perkins (1840-1872) March 1838

Peters Family

James (about 1750-February 8, 1828) married Lucy Parker (about 1750-) on March 29, 1768 in Sussex County Virginia

Their children were:

James (1785-) married Rebecca Boddie (February 7, 1791-

Their children were:

Susannah Hill (December 31, 1810-November 9, 1866) married William Arthur (July 12, 1809-1882) September 20, 1831

Thomas Hill (October 29, 1812-September 9, 1883) married Ann Eliza Glasgow (-1842) 1837 married Sarah J. Irion (-1859) 1846

George Boddie (1814-April 29, 1889) married married Narcissa Williams (1819-March 20, 1840) May 9, 1839, married Evelina Louisa McNeal (July 26, 1818-October 20, 1855) July 29, 1841, married Jessie McKissack (January 3, 1838-1921) June 1, 1858

John Buxton (March 15, 1817-July 10, 1864) married Paralee Jackson (September 2, 1820-June 2, 1866) November 11, 1840

Ann Elizabeth (June 15, 1819-February 25. 1912 in

Marshall, TX) married Benjamin Franklin Young (August 10, 1810-May 24, 1863) November 21, 1840

Lucy (1851-) married John B. Cobb

Mary Caroline (1827-1852) married Robert Archibald Burton (January 20, 1822-1872) November 1, 1848

James(1828-)

Rebecca (May 9, 1833-September 1899) married James Ronald Chalmers (January 12, 1831-April 1898) June 6, 1854

Ellen Pauline (1832-) married Dr. William Green Wright ( )

Dr. George Boddie Peters (1814-April 29, 1889) married Narcissa Williams (1819-March 20, 1840) in May 9, 1839 in Hardeman County, Tennessee

Their child was:

Thomas (March 20, 1840-July 1840)

Dr. George Boddie Peters (1814-April 29, 1889) married Evelina Louisa McNeal (July 26, 1818-October 20, 1855) on July 29, 1841 in Hardeman County, Tennessee

Their children were:

Thomas McNeal (May 21, 1842-April 9, 1866)
Irene (February 27, 1844-July 22, 1845)
James Arthur (December 1845-January 31, 1891)
Clara Polk (January 20-November 30, 1917)
George Boddie, Jr. (January 11, 1850-December 8, 1906) married Katie Bell Greenlaw (1855-March 12, 1897) June 13, 1872

Their children were:

Evelyn McNeal (May 10, 1873-1954) married Wyatt

C. Estes (March 30, 1870-) March 1891 Married Charles N. Burch (1868-1938) March 1916

Mignon "Minnie" Greenlaw (January 31, 1875-1939) married Elisha Eldridge Wright (July 25, 1871-January 22, 1912) December 18, 1895

Madge Claire (January 19, 1877-December 1878)

Kate Bell (May 28, 1880-1921) married Daniel C. Gillett

Clara Polk (October 6,1882-October 14, 1975) married Henry C. Pfeiffer

James Arthur (October 19, 1884-April 24, 1934) married Bessie

Hadeaux (August 1890-September 2, 1919) April 3, 1908

George Boddie III (April 24, 1887-1923) married Mary Young

Mary Eliza (December 20, 1853-November 21, 1855)

Samuel McNeal (September 13, 1854-August 26, 1855)

Dr. George Boddie Peters (1814-April 29, 1889) married Jessie Helen McKissack (January 3, 1838-July 18, 1921) on June 1, 1858 in Spring Hill, Tennessee

Their children were:

Harry (December 20, 1858-January 17, 1858)
William McKissack (March 16, 1859-April 6, 1885)
Lucy Mary (November 11, 1861-October 24, 1874)

Medora Wharton (January 26, 1864-October 26, 1931) married Henry Joyner Lenow (1854-July 23, 1925) October 22, 1884

Their children were:

Helene Jessie (May 6, 1886-June 27, 1960) married

George Myers Guerin (May 26, 1886-October 5, 1922) September 25, 1922

Francis Jesep (December 25, 1888-April1, 1964) married Josephanie Carr (December 13, 1888-September 15, 1967)

Lila (October 17, 1889-August 15, 1957) married Edmund B. Willins (July 5, 1881-December 2, 1934)

Henry Joyner, Jr. (July 20, 1891-April 18, 1952) married Ruby Stevens (August 12, 1909-December 20, 1993) December 31, 1931
Divorced 1939

Columbus Bierce (July 20, 1891-April 1964) married Mary Sue Bolinger about 1916

Kate Thomson (1893-October 24, 1921) married George Myers Guerin (May 26, 1886-October 5, 1922) 1917

Arundel (February 7, 1895-January 1, 1970) married Margaret Mivelez (July 10, 1900-October 3, 1986)

Medora (1897-November 24, 1990) married Cary W. Salter (June 29, 1888-March 1, 1968)

Nell R. (March 13, 1899-July 1974) married Harold H. Hansen (November 15, 1881-1967)

Louise (December 18, 1901-Died as baby)

Lucy H. (1902-April 2, 1961)

William McKissack (1904-August 11, 1959)

Flora Maury (March 1, 1906-June 14, 1994) married Van B. Martin (January 28, 1904-February 17, 1975)

Robert A. (November 6, 1908-January 16, 1975) married Gladys Wheeler (1902-June 16, 1984)

Kate Chalmers (December 23, 1873-March 27, 1943) married Ezra Wallace Holden (1868-1938) April 17, 1895 divorced 1901

Their child was:

William Robert Holden (May 25, 1899-April 8, 1985) married Virginia

Robert Edward Lee Peters March 9, 1876-April 19, 1928) married Emma Clark (1883-December 20, 1934)

Their children were:

Emma Lee Peters (1917-1989) married Tom Barrow
Virginia Clark (1919-1983) married Robert Harper

Van Dorn Family

Earl Van Dorn (September 17, 1820-May 7, 1863) married Caroline Godbold (1827-January 19, 1876) December 23, 1843

Their children were:

Olivia Van Dorn (April 1, 1852-February 4, 1878) married Frank Aubrey Lumsden (October 1845-January 1, 1911) October 8, 1868

Their children were:

Lily E. (July 8, 1869-)
Lucy Caroline (October 18, 1873-)
Frank Aubrey (January 17, 1875-)
Tunstall (January 23, 1878-)

Earl Van Dorn (July 27, 1854-April 3, 1884)

Martha Goodbread (1836-abt. 1870) Never married to Van Dorn (Later married a Bird)

Their children were:

Percy Van Dorn (1857-September 1879)

Lammie Belle Van Dorn (October 1, 1859-July 1, 1930)
   Married James T. Carr (February 5, 1850-May 11, 1940)
   August 4, 1877

Their Children were:

Itasca (February 1878-June 7, 1964)
Daisie (November 1881-September 5, 1941)
Orville Percy (March 1891-January 23, 1962)

Douglas Van Dorn (November 1, 1861-August 22, 1906)
   married Lou Asie Heathcock (November 1, 1861-) June
   3, 1880

Their children were:

William (March 11, 1881-June 24, 1976)
Stella (1883-1883)
Ella Mae (November 5, 1885-January 9, 1929)
Percy Frederick (October 1, 1890-January 26, 1958)
Mattie (June 1891-December 9, 1918)
Lorena (February 2, 1893-October 19, 1985)
Walter Douglas (August 23, 1894-February 6. 1926)
Ollie Douglas (May 4, 1896-August 23, 1906)
Lillian Florence (August 1897-May 12, 1981)
Maude Myrtle (September 9, 1900-December 3, 1989)
Etta (December 29, 1903-May 8, 1925)
Ada Cleo (December 10, 1906-March 1, 2000)

*Information taken from cemetery records, family history, family Bibles, census records, death certificates, marriage records, newspaper articles, DAR applications, and Bodie, John Thomas *Boddie and Allied Families* (United States 1918).

Epilog

The McKissack family home that was built by William still stands in the down town area of Spring Hill, Tennessee, and is privately owned.

White Hall, the house where General Van Dorn first had his headquarters in Spring Hill, is privately owned and still stands today on Duplex Road. It is open by appointment. The Peters' home that Jessie inherited from her father that was located on Kedron Pike that could be seen from the Martin Cheairs' home burned in 1957.

The Martin Cheairs' home, the second location of General Van Dorn's headquarters and ultimate death, is part of the Tennessee Children's Home. When Martin Cheairs died, the house and about 57 acres were sold to the Spring Hill Male College that became Branham and Hughes Academy. At that time, the house became known as Ferguson Hall. It became a military academy in 1918 and was considered an excellent educational institution; however, it had to be closed during the depression. In 1934 the property was deeded to the Trustees of the Tennessee Orphan's Home and later became known as the Tennessee Children's Home. The house has been restored and is open by appointment.

Rippavilla or Rippa Villa, the home of Susan McKissack, sister of Jessie McKissack Peters and Nathaniel Cheairs, brother of William Cheairs, is open to the public as an historic site. It is the location where General John Bell Hood and his general officers ate breakfast before the Battle of Franklin. Five of the generals were killed in battle before the end of the day.

The Grace Episcopal Church that stands on land that was once the garden of the McKissack home still stands and continues to have services for the small congregation.

Dr. George B. Peters was buried in the southern part of the family plot in Elmwood Cemetery in Memphis. Jessie H. Peters is buried to his left. To Jessie's left is Mrs. J. H. Peters. According to *Obituaries from Tennessee Newspapers*, by Jill Garrett, 1980, "This is correctly the burial for A. C. McKissack, brother of Mrs. J. H. Peters." She had a brother by the name of Alexander Cagle who would have been about 68 years old in 1898 when the burial took place on September 28, 1898. A graduate of Yale, he had been a wealthy farmer near Holly Springs in Marshall County, Mississippi prior to the war. By 1880 he was listed as a manufacturer in Pulaski, Tennessee. He visited Jessie quite often in Memphis, and on this occasion, he had a heart attack in her home and died. Behind her is a small simple stone that reads:

> Medora Peters Lenow
> Jan   26   1865 (This is incorrect for she was born in 1864.)
> Oct   26   1931

There is an empty plot behind Dr. Peters, and behind that area is buried

> Kate Peters
> Holden
> Died Mar. 26, 1943
> Age 70 years

To her left is William W. Peters, and to his left is Lucy Peters. There are no tombstones to mark the graves of the others. It was stated by family members that because of all the publicity that surrounded Jessie and Dr. Peters, no stone was erected for them. Medora and Kate's stones are very simple. Medora's husband Henry is buried on the opposite side of the cemetery that has a very large family stone where his parents are buried. He is buried behind them, and the grave of his daughter Lucy is near.

In November 1899, Emily Van Dorn Miller was living in Washington, D.C., and with the assistance of her son T. Marshall Miller, had General Earl Van Dorn's remains moved and sent by rail to Wintergreen Cemetery in Port Gibson, Mississippi. Before the reburial next to their father, the casket was opened to find the body in a gray Confederate uniform of a major general. The belt, buckles, and epaulettes were undamaged, and the soft golden curls were around his shoulders. He was buried in a north south direction as his father so he could see his boyhood home.

The ThyssenKrupp Steel USA Company built a $4.2 billion plant for steel and stainless steel processing in the Calvert, Alabama, area that was built over several acres. An archeological dig was done in the area of the Godbold house that burned in the 1920s. Ancestors of Dr. William T. Webb's family who purchased the property after the war indicated that the house had a mahogany staircase, marble, many items from Europe, and was a very fine house. Since Dr. Webb had an office in Mobile, he traveled back home on weekends to be with his family. William Cumberland bought the house for his family, and he lived in the house until he died. The house burned down sometime after his death in 1916. The cemetery was close to a hill that could be seen from the Godbold house. All the graves in the Family Cemetery were removed and placed in storage until reburial in a new site. The ThyssenKrupp Company is located over all the original Godbold and Van Dorn cemetery sites.

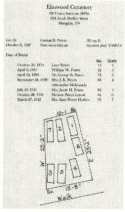

Peters' family plot in Elm wood Cemetery, Memphis, TN.

Peters' family plot in Elmwood Cemetery, Memphis, TN. Only two graves are marked because of adverse publicity.

Medora's marker in Peters' family plot. Birth date should be January 26, 1864.

Kate and Medora's graves are the only ones marked in Peters' plot in Elmwood Cemetery, Memphis, TN.

Lenow Family plot where Medora's husband Henry is buried. Their daughter Lucy who suffered from epilepsy is also here. The family plot is on the opposite side of the cemetery where Peters plot is located.